Strategy for Survival

James Thompson

for

Survival

A Plan for Church Renewal from Hebrews

D1383128

JOURNEY BOOKS

An SPC Publication
Austin, Texas 78765

Edited by Garner Roberts and Roger Hornbaker
Cover designed by Tom Williams

Printed in the U.S.A.
Library of Congress Catalog Card Number 79-67274
ISBN 0-8344-0113-4
5 4 3 2 1

Contents

1

Reviving
a Tired Church

"I appeal to you brethren, bear with my word of exhortation."

Hebrews 13:22

Tourists who travel to cities in Europe or America are often told that they "must" see the great historic churches. The Notre Dame and Canterbury cathedrals are majestic witnesses to the intense devotion of the Middle Ages. But people look at them in the same way they see the Louvre and British Museum. These cathedrals are monuments to the past. Like museums, they tell us about a past discovered only through its lifeless relics. They tell us little about a living, vital faith. The intense devotion once represented by these monuments belongs to history.

Many people believe Christianity faces the same

inevitable decline today. Churches, we are often told, will become museums. Christianity will live on in small groups of people, but the vitality will be gone.

People base these pessimistic predictions on reports that say religion is declining in American life. Sociologists tell about a startling contradiction: people are as religious as they were a generation ago, but they go to church less. When George Gallup conducts a poll on common beliefs about God or Christ, the statistics reveal the same high percentages as always. But fewer people attend church. One study concluded, "It used to be that people went to church and didn't think much about religious matters. Now people think about religious matters and don't much go to church."[1]

Church membership statistics in the United States reveal general trends about the vitality of religion. For some years, Gallup polls asked a sample of adults if they had attended church during the previous week. Affirmative answers are sometimes inflated because the people tend to answer as they think they should answer. Therefore, church attendance was probably overestimated. But the general trend is unmistakable. Although 49 percent of adults reported church attendance in a given week in 1955 and again in 1958, there has been a steady drop to 40 percent in the years after 1971.[2] The chief decline in church attendance came among young adults, ages 21-29. Polls indicate their attendance declined 20 percent from 1958 to 1971.

Such studies leave many people understandably disturbed about religious involvement. We cannot ignore these statistics, and we cannot deny that we live in a culture where involvement in church life is less popular than it once was. It was one thing to expect a high degree of involvement when participation in church life was considered popular. It is quite another to motivate people in a culture that is increasingly secularized. Thus we should be concerned about growing tendencies toward secularization and their implications for all congregations.

We cannot gather statistical data to measure the health of local congregations everywhere. Undoubtedly, there are signs of vitality in many congregations, such as impressive budgets, large Sunday school programs, bus ministries, and patterns of growth. In many instances the vitality can be seen where an extraordinary number of people are actively involved in at least one ministry of the local church.

Many of these indicators may point to genuine signs of life in the church. But some impressive statistics may reflect nothing more than a pattern of mobility where there is a concentration of resources in only a few places. And there are more visible signs of the declining health of local churches. Some young people find the church boring and go elsewhere. Church attendance is dropping, and it is harder to raise money for the church. We also have reason to be concerned when people, looking for a church home or a vital faith, turn to unusual cults or substitute religions. In many cities church membership declines as the population increases.

Finding Resources For Our Task:
A Biblical Approach

These disturbing signs do not necessarily point to an irreversible decline in the church. In fact, students of the Bible know there have been many other periods of decline in the past when faithful people considered their cause a failure. If we worry about the future of the church, we should recall that the Bible is not a story of triumph after triumph. Discouragement overcame the children of Israel shortly after their triumphant exodus from Egypt. Perhaps an experienced sociologist or pollster would have forecast the death of the movement then. Stories of the prophets include more accounts of desperation and discouragement than victory. Elijah complained, during his confrontation with Ahab and Jezebel, that "the people of Israel have forsaken thy covenant, thrown down thy altars and slain thy prophets with the sword; and I even I only am left" (1 Kings 19:10). He made the statement after a great victory over the prophets of Baal. But Elijah saw before him the imminent doom of God's people. And this desperation sent him to Mount Horeb to seek his religious roots.

"We have been more successful in providing momentary diversions than in providing on-going renewal of the church."

Ezekiel's vision of the valley of dry bones reflected the apparently hopeless condition of the people of God (Ezek. 37). The prophet looked out over the valley and heard a voice ask the question, "Can these bones live?" (Ezek. 37:3). The bones were symbolic of the spiritual condition of the Israelite exiles.

Jesus' ministry did not always look like a success story. There were instances when "many of his disciples drew back and no longer went about with him" (John 6:66). Thus, there have always been periods of decline among the people of God.

What resources do we have to bring life to a tired community? Of course, it is God who ultimately works to bring life to the church. In Ezekiel's vision of the dry bones, it was God's spirit, or "breath," which brought the bones back to life. But Ezekiel was also given a task (Ezek. 37:4) of prophesying to the bones. We must revitalize weary congregations in the same way. But it is not easy to know what to say. In the past (and in many places today) periodic "revivals" or "meetings" were tried to achieve renewal. In many instances, these occasions were very useful in stimulating the church to greater service. Meetings, campaigns, and other special programs indicate our awareness that communities do grow tired and that one of our great needs is to find the resources for renewal.

Something is missing in our search for ways to renew the church. We have been more successful in providing momentary diversions than in providing on going renewal of the church. If our attempts to restore the vitality of the church are successful, they will deal with the continuing problem, and they will also be built on a biblical model. Our attempts to provide vitality too often ignore our biblical heritage.

There is one book in the New Testament addressed to the problem of awakening a tired church. The epistle to the Hebrews provides our best biblical model for awakening churches. The readers of Hebrews shared many of our basic problems. We can learn something very useful for

9

our congregations if we study how the Hebrews writer responded to problems which are similar to our own.

The Perspective Of Hebrews

Hebrews may not look like a book on church renewal. Many people remember only the often complicated arguments in Hebrews. Indeed, we notice first that Hebrews consists of a series of arguments comparing Jesus Christ with aspects of Old Testament life in order to say that Christ is "better" (note the use of the word "better" in 1:4, 8:6, 9:23). It has been argued, consequently, that the purpose of the book was to show people who were considering a return to Judaism that Christianity is superior to Judaism.

But Hebrews is not only an argument. One of the most striking aspects of the book is its different style and tone. Most books of the New Testament are letters written in response to specific problems of ancient churches. But, as the first lines of Hebrews indicate, the book is not a letter. Other letters begin by naming the author and his readers, but Hebrews does not. We do not know the author or the readers. The author never identifies himself. And we call the readers "Hebrews" because early Christians assumed that only "Hebrews" could understand the many arguments based on the Old Testament.

The author calls it a "word of exhortation" (Heb. 13:22). That indicates that the author's intent was not primarily to debate or engage in abstract arguments. He intended it as a sermon. The expression "word of exhortation" appears in one other instance in the New Testament (Acts 13:15).

10

It applies to a synagogue sermon. Thus Hebrews is a unique work. It is the only recorded sermon we have from the early church intended for Christians. We have many examples in Acts of missionary sermons, but Hebrews is a sermon to the church. The book is filled with exhortations to show us that, like a good preacher, the author knew his audience well. He refers often to the situation of the readers, and in many places he appeals to them with the personal address, "Let us . . . " (4:14, 16; 6:1; 10:22). Hebrews is a sermon, not a lecture.

From these exhortations in Hebrews, we know that the readers faced problems very similar to our own. The readers were in danger of committing apostasy (Heb. 6:6). Although they had been Christians long enough to have developed spiritual depth and insight, the author says they were "dull of hearing" and still required milk rather than solid food (5:12). Some of them began to drop out of the assembly (Heb. 10:25). Hebrews is the only book of the New Testament to address itself to that problem, apparently because other communities had not yet faced the same problem. According to Hebrews 10:36, the most fundamental need of these Christians is endurance. Hebrews 12:12 presents a vivid image of people on a pilgrimage who now have "dropping hands and weak knees."

If we pay close attention to the exhortations in Hebrews, we get a picture of the original readers. There is nothing specifically said about strange doctrines which made their way into the church. The author's direct references to their situation leave us with the impression that the readers were tired after a generation of commitment to the cause of Christ.

Causes Of Apathy

We are not sure what caused the sense of weariness that tempted some to "neglect such a great salvation" (Heb. 2:3). We only notice the author's uncertainty over whether they will finish the course (note the "if" clauses in 3:6, 14). Perhaps there were Christians who had made their initial commitment in a moment of great congregational excitement and were simply caught up in the prevailing mood. It is possible that they had expected these peak experiences to be a daily affair and that they were totally unprepared for a return to the routine affairs of church life. It is also possible that the readers were first converted at a time when everyone expected the Lord to return soon. They had been able to keep up the high level of commitment for a while, but they could not maintain their enthusiasm year after year. And it is possible that they lived in a town where there was considerable competition from new and exotic cults. Perhaps the worship services of the church seemed very ordinary when compared to other places where "things were happening." Perhaps some, wanting to be where the action was, were inclined to follow the newest fads.

Whatever the reasons for the readers' "drift" (2:1), the author faced the difficult task of encouraging them to "lift up their drooping hands and weak knees" (12:12) and of calling them back to the assembly.

How do you go about the task of calling people back to their original commitment? We should be vitally interested in the message of Hebrews because we share the same task which the author faced. The author was a preacher, and his task was to stimulate and encourage. We can learn something very important from his way of handling the matter.

One very noticeable feature of this "word of exhortation" is the space devoted to the exposition of scripture. We might expect a "word of exhortation" to consist almost entirely of urgent demands and appeals. But the exhortations are interspersed with arguments based on scripture. For instance, chapter 1 is a series of biblical quotations intended to demonstrate that the Son of God is "better than angels" (1:4). This argument then becomes the basis for the exhortation to his tired readers not to "neglect such a great salvation" (2:3). The affirmations in chapter 2 about the humanity of Jesus provide the background for the author's statement that the one who has been tempted "is able to help those who are tempted" (2:18). The fact that Christ is the high priest in the ideal sanctuary (5:1–10:18) provides the basis for appealing to the readers to "have confidence to enter the sanctuary by the blood of Jesus" (10:19). In fact, words of exhortation are always closely connected to the teaching material.

A Model Sermon

The author of Hebrews is probably the model preacher. This combination of teaching with exhortation shows us what is really necessary for church renewal. A church cannot be stimulated forever on exhortation alone. We grow immune to constant appeals, regardless of how fervent they are. If we are to maintain a vital faith, we need roots in a faith which appeals to our minds. We need careful examination of the Bible that will allow us to grow.

The author of Hebrews has provided us a model "word of exhortation." His arguments from scripture appeal to our minds and allow us to grow. His exposition of scripture always ends in an appeal to the church to consider the greatness of its salvation and to maintain its identity. He knows that genuine renewal includes not only momentary stimulation, but addresses the needs of the church from one generation to another.

A church cannot be stimulated forever on exhortation alone.

Undoubtedly, one of the reasons many people find Christianity easy to give up is that they have never understood its richness and wealth. We try to preserve their interest by neglecting those very areas which we anticipate that others will find unappealing. But the reason the author of Hebrews devotes his time to those subjects which appear to be difficult or "hard to explain" (5:11) is that he wants us to remember what a "great salvation" (2:3) we have. Those who appreciate its richness will hesitate before they throw it away.

In Hebrews 10:23 the author counsels his tired church, "Let us hold fast the confession of our hope without wavering, for he who promised is faithful." Undoubtedly we will not "hold fast" to the faith "without wavering" if we are unconvinced that our faith rests on a solid foundation. We will see no reason to endure the frustrations, discouragements, and disappointments that sometimes go with the Christian life unless our faith provides the solid foundation for our lives. Hebrews has the unique structure of alternating great arguments and affirmations with appeals to a tired church. The arguments demonstrate that we have a faith to which we can hold "without wavering" and a reason for enduring the frustrations and anguish of going on with the Christian life.

We can learn much by observing the method of the author of Hebrews in calling his people back to a life of service. We need to realize the seriousness and urgency of awakening whole congregations to their responsibilities. But we also need to remind people, as the author of Hebrews does, that there are solid reasons for remaining faithful, for ours is a "great salvation."

This great salvation, according to the author, is an "anchor of the soul" (6:19). The image of the "anchor," which appears in no other place in the Bible, is an appropriate word for the very thing the church needs in a time of change and uncertainty. It suggests that our faith provides a source of security which will prevent us from drifting aimlessly. The religion sections of news magazines provide abundant evidence that many people are looking for an "anchor" at the very time when traditional religions are unattractive. In the place of the traditional religions, some people find their anchor in political dogmas which are supposed to redeem the world. Such dogmas have become substitute religions. In the 1970s we have seen the growth of various other religious alternatives. Many young people have been attracted to the religions of the East. Others have tried to find salvation in the newer cults which have had extraordinary growth. For others, the human potential movement has become a substitute religion. Transcendental Meditation, est, group encounter sessions, and many other versions of this movement offer people the chance to become a new person and to find inner peace. They are searching for an anchor for their lives.

This book is written in the conviction that Hebrews is more than an ancient document to read for historical purposes. It is directed not just to a tired community of the past. It is a "word of exhortation" for us today.

---

[1]Robert Wuthnow and Charles Glock, "The Religious Experience," *Psychology Today* (December 1973), p. 14.
[2]Harvey Seifert, *New Power for the Church* (Philadelphia: Westminster Press, 1976).

2

Realizing Our
Great Salvation

"*How shall we escape if we neglect such a great salvation?*"

Hebrews 1:1–2:4; 3:1-6

In the hymn "The Church's One Foundation," the people of God are portrayed as living through "toil and tribulation" which involves oppression from the outside and schism and heresy from within. If a hymn writer of today wanted to portray the struggles of God's people in the twentieth century, he would probably describe it another way. In the western world, our problem is not "toil and tribulation" from the outside. Nor is our major problem that we are "by heresies distrest." The problem in the latter part of the twentieth century is that the church encounters indifference from the outside and apathy from its own people.

Threatening Voices

It is not easy to know what to say to people

whose struggle is not against persecution, but rather against apathy. The apathy has been created by a culture that considers Christianity tired and bereft of anything to say. It is discouraging to notice that people who are tired of the Christian message do not merely give up on religion. They turn to substitute religions. For some people, political ideology is the new "savior." It can build its own "new heaven and new earth," especially when it consumes our energy and promises its own glorious future. In recent times, a surprising number of people have turned to new forms and theories of psychology in order to "find themselves." Psychology is, of course, a useful discipline in many circumstances. But some forms can also serve as a substitute religion, complete with a promise of release from guilt and a salvation that is found when we discover our essential selves. In many places, especially among the affluent, salvation is sought everywhere but in church. Many other worthwhile areas can become religions if they are treated as the "ultimate concern" of their followers.

If the church is threatened today by the claims of other voices, it is not the first time. As early as the epistle to the Hebrews, the church was in danger of being "led away by diverse and strange teachings" (13:9). The church has always been tempted to try to revitalize itself by accommodating those other voices which become popular. Some people have always tried to show the basic compatibility of Christianity with whatever political system was popular. Germans during the Third Reich tried to show its compatibility with National Socialism; Marxists tried to show its compatibility with Marxism; capitalists have tried to show that

18

Christianity supports the free enterprise system. Today we are tempted to revitalize the church by importing the latest theories of psychology or sociology or human development and combining them with a few Christian terms. It is tempting to find our relevance to the outside world by giving it a message that fits popular tastes.

To a certain extent, this desire to speak the language of the people is understandable, for behind it there is the desire to communitate. From the days of the apostles until now, Christians have always recognized the need for "becoming all things to all men." Anyone who has tried to proclaim the gospel in another culture knows that the story has to be told in such a way that the listeners will understand.

There is danger, however, in accommodation. The message may be so adapted to the tastes of the audience that the church is left with no clear voice. We are tempted to think that interest in the life of the church can be revived if only the message affirms what is already popular.

A Clear Voice (1:1-4)

In one sense, the author of Hebrews has probably accomodated his message to his audience. This book is unique in its style and method of presentation. Probably this difference of style is the result of the author's attempt to address an audience different from those addressed in other books. What is most striking about this book is its elegant Greek style, perhaps the best style in the New Testament. Readers have observed for centuries that the author of Hebrews uses a wider philosophical vocabulary than anyone else in the New Testament. The writer declares the gospel in terms that could be accepted by educated people of the Greek world. Indeed, the first four verses of Hebrews are written with a distinctive literary style. The first sentence has an alliteration that is unmatched in the New Testament (five words of the first sentence begin with the letter "p" in Greek). Even in English these verses have a striking rhetorical impact. Thus the author does accommodate himself to his readers.

But there is one point at which the author is uncompromising. He wants his readers to recognize that Jesus Christ is not just one voice among many. The first four verses summarize what the author says in the doctrinal portions of the book: Jesus Christ is God's final and ultimate voice. As the entire book suggests, we are capable of placing our hopes in a variety of spokesmen. We are tempted to make Jesus Christ one voice among others. Consequently, Hebrews is composed of a series of comparisons. Jesus is compared to angels (chs. 1-2), Moses (3:1-6), Joshua (4:8), and the levitical priests (7:1–10:18). But the author is always uncompromising: the Christian faith rests, not on the belief that Jesus is one voice among others, but on the belief that he is God's final word. At this point there is no accommodation to the tastes of the audience.

What did weary Christians need to hear to help preserve their Christian identity? They needed more than a pep-talk. They needed to know about the essential facts of the Christian faith, the very facts to which they had confessed at their baptism.

Perhaps the beautiful words of the first four verses of the book are actually the very words which the readers had once confessed at the beginning of their Christian lives. More than once the author reminds his readers of their "confession" (3:1, 10:23). It is a confession that they are summoned to "consider" and "hold fast."

The renewal of the church does not begin when the members repeat words which are popular and acceptable in their culture. It begins with the reminder that the church lives by a confession of faith that will not allow Jesus Christ to be one voice among others. Before the author appeals to his readers to keep the faith (2:1-4), he reminds them of the greatness of the faith that they have already confessed: God's final word has been declared in Jesus Christ.

Essential Beliefs

Churches have had their share of disputes in attempting to summarize the essential features of the Christian faith. Extensive creeds have been drawn up to determine what is the most important affirmation of Christianity. For the author of Hebrews, the essential fact is the place of Jesus Christ in the world. In Hebrews 1:1-4 the writer uses one of the favorite terms of the entire epistle to describe Jesus Christ: He is God's Son (1:2, 4; 3:6; 5:5, 8) and final word. To say that Jesus is the Son of God is to describe His unique place in the world and in salvation. None of the other spokesmen has ever been like him. We may appreciate other voices. We may learn from many teachers. But, as the author of Hebrews tells us, the last word has come in God's Son, who is different from all the rest.

"Renewal begins with going back to the essential affirmations of our faith: the recognition that Jesus is unlike any rival."

The author of Hebrews then lists six features which make Jesus unique, which distinguish him from all other beings. The words sound like the first chapter of John's gospel and the beautiful passage in Colossians 1:15-20 which describes the unique status of Jesus. These six features describing Jesus Christ summarize all that the author wants to say about Jesus Christ in the rest of the book. The story of Jesus may be divided, as this passage tells us, into three stages: Jesus' role in creation ("whom he has appointed the heir of all things, through whom also he created the world. He reflects the glory of God and bears the very stamp of his nature, upholding the universe by the word of his power"), his earthly life as redeemer ("when he made purification for sins . . ."), and his exalted status at the right hand of God ("he sat down at the right hand of the majesty on high"). Throughout the book, these are the essential facts of the Christian faith. Without the story of Jesus' earthly life, Christianity would be reduced to myth. Consequently, the book reminds us that Jesus was a man (2:17, 4:15, 5:8). Without his exaltation to God's right hand (8:1), Christianity would be only a human adventure.

The words of 1:1-4 describe Jesus in his full dignity. They apply to no one else. These verses tell why he is "better" than the angels (1:4) and Moses (3:1-6). He is not one voice among many.

The author begins in 1:1-4 with affirmations about the dignity of Jesus Christ. The author knows that his listeners will never pay the price of enduring if Jesus has merely brought a message that is available elsewhere. If the words of Jesus can be found among other spokesmen, there is no reason to endure. Consequently, renewal begins with going back to the essential affirmations of our faith: the recognition that Jesus is unlike any rival.

Arguments From Scripture (1:5-13)

When the Hebrews' writer states his claim about Jesus Christ, he always refers back to his Bible, the Old Testament. Undoubtedly he knew that Christianity would not survive unless it was firmly rooted in scripture. Claims which were not based on scripture would have been empty. Thus in Hebrews 1:5-13 he supports the majestic affirmations of 1:1-4 by demonstrating from scripture that Christ is "better than angels" (1:4). He quotes seven passages from the Old Testament, mostly from the Psalms, describing the unique status of Jesus Christ. It is as if the entire Old Testament is the story of Jesus Christ.

How is Christ unique? The author has not arranged these quotations in a haphazard way. He has chosen scriptures which illustrate the major themes of the book. The first two passages (Ps. 2:7, 2 Sam. 7:14), for instance, reaffirm that Jesus is God's unique Son. The third passage (1:6) quotes Deuteronomy 32:43 and suggests that angels recognize his unique status. Verses 7-12 demonstrate *how* Jesus is superior to angels. There is a recurring emphasis on the fact that Jesus Christ is now eternal and unchangeable. In 1:8, for instance, we read that the Old Testament affirms that His throne is "for ever and ever." In 1:10-11 we learn that the Son who created the world (1:2-3) stands above its change and decay. "They will perish, but thou remainest" (1:11). Nature will be subject to change, but the Son always remains the same (1:12). Thus the most significant fact about the exalted status of Jesus is that He, unlike other spokesmen, is always the same.

This "sameness" of Jesus Christ is a major theme in Hebrews. Indeed, one of the most memorable passages of the entire book comes near the end: "Jesus Christ is the same yesterday, today, and forever" (13:8). According to 7:24, he is the great high priest who "continues forever."

If Jesus Christ is the One among all other leaders who remains "the same," it would be absurd to turn elsewhere for salvation. But both ancient and modern people have tried to revitalize the church by accommodating the Christian message to popular tastes, not by reaffirming that Jesus Christ is God's final word. We are tempted to show how Christianity agrees with a certain political philosophy or secular cause. The church may become the place where we offer courses in "pop psychology" or self-awareness, as if the answer to our problem is to be more "with it." The epistle to the Hebrews has a different response. The answer for a tiring church, Hebrews says, is to reaffirm our essential confession: Jesus Christ is God's final word to us. All other causes will disappear.

The growth of new religious movements in recent years demonstrates that people, in a world filled with change and insecurity, are looking for an anchor for their lives. The rate of change disturbs people. They watch as the values, traditions, and standards of the past collapse. The author of Hebrews knew that we find this anchor only when we discover the One who remains the same, not in accommodating the faith to the prevailing tastes.

A Word Of Exhortation (2:1-4)

When we come to the "therefore" of 2:1, we begin to understand why a book that was intended to awaken a weary church devotes all of chapter 1 to the reaffirmation of the church's faith. In 2:1-4, the author demonstrates that his weighty arguments of chapter 1 have a practical result for the life of the church. Now he sounds like a concerned preacher. He addresses his audience in the first person. "We must pay the closer attention to what we have heard, lest we drift away from it" (2:1). "How shall we escape if we neglect such a great salvation (2:3)?" The personal address suggests that the author is a preacher who identifies with the needs of the church. As he says, "we" have heard something which needs to be taken seriously.

Why has the author devoted a chapter to weighty arguments before addressing his audience personally? He sees his community, like communities we have seen, in the process of "drifting away" (2:1). The image of "drifting away" is a nautical term. It suggests a ship on the sea which drifts along without anchor. It is as if he had said, "Christians are like a ship. Without an anchor they drift aimlessly along." Or, as 2:3 says, they will "neglect" (*ameleō*) their "great salvation." The word for "neglect" (*ameleō*) was often used in the New Testament for people who had no appreciation for a valuable item (1 Tim. 4:14), such as when the guests in Jesus' parable of the banquet "made light" (*ameleō*) of the invitation (Matt. 22:5).

The great affirmations of chapter 1 have thus preceded the exhortation in 2:1-4 because the author wants his readers to recognize what a "great salvation" they have. It might not be a tragedy to "drift away" from or "neglect" a new fad. But a great salvation is too important to be thrown away. It needs to be taken seriously. The author says, "Therefore we must pay the closer attention to what we have heard." "What we have heard" is too important to be taken lightly.

The church may respond to apathy among its people today with a bit of embarrassment over the content of its message. "What we have heard" sometimes seems to be like a record worn smooth after too much playing. The Christian story may appear to be in need of accommodation to new ideas. But the author of Hebrews declares that our hope lies in taking seriously the "great salvation" which we have heard. As he suggests in 2:3-4, it has been validated not only in the life of Jesus, but also in the lives of countless others.

Renewal in the church begins not by pushing our original confession of faith into the background, but by taking seriously the words confessed at baptism. The renewal of the church today cannot avoid a return to the one story which serves as an anchor for our lives.

3

Looking to the Pioneer

"But we see Jesus . . ."

Hebrews 2:5-18

There is much realism in Hebrews' description of the Christian life as a journey toward a distant goal. The image may not be one we would have chosen because it suggests the weariness and declining enthusiasm that accompanies a long pilgrimage. We might prefer images of joy and exhilaration which go with believing. But the author of Hebrews knew a community that had lost its enthusiasm. It was in danger of "throwing away" its confidence (10:35) and of "committing apostasy" (6:6). Like people who have traveled a long way, they now have "drooping hands" and "weak knees" (12:12). Therefore, the author was faced with the task of encouraging tired pilgrims not to quit before they reached the goal.

27

This task is similar to our own. One of our most serious problems is encouraging people not to "drift away" (2:1). We must deal with people who appear to be tired after an extended journey. They look back upon years of dutiful service as if it were an excessively long journey. New promotional schemes and programs are of limited value in maintaining a declining enthusiasm. We need something more extensive than an occasional pep rally.

Most of us know people who have difficulty with the long journey of a Christian life. Many people are disappointed when the excitement of the first days of the Christian life wears off and becomes a routine of discipline and obligation. Many of us are unprepared for the disappointments and weariness of a lifetime of commitment.

Maintaining Our Intensity

What can we do to maintain our direction and intensity? The first chapter of Hebrews responds to the reader's temptation to drift away. By paying attention to our "great salvation" (2:1), we have the resources to hold firm in our commitments. This "great salvation" consists in the reflections on the exalted status of Jesus Christ mentioned in chapter 1. The Christ whom we confessed when we began this pilgrimage is no ordinary person. He reflects God's glory (1:3), and now he has achieved a status that makes him greater than angels (1:4). Everything else in the creation may change, but he is forever "the same" (1:12).

The author tells a tired community that survival depends on whether we know Jesus. To many of us, this is either a waste of time or the business of a few professionals. Our culture has an activist bias which often prefers action over reflection. And while the church can never cease its activity, it will die if it does not consider the fundamental question: who is Jesus? We are tempted to find our security in fads which promise to restore interest and vitality to the church. But there is no vitality unless we know Jesus and find our security in Him.

"Our culture has an activist bias which often prefers action over reflection."

There is security in knowing that he, among many conflicting voices, abides forever (Heb. 1:12). We know that we can rely on him. But knowing Jesus does not stop with knowing about his majesty, as expressed in Hebrews 1. We who struggle on the long pilgrimage, with our temptations to drift away, want to know about his power and eternity. And we want to know also if he understands our temptations to give up. Is he far removed from the questions which disturb us? This is answered in Hebrews 2:5-18.

Jesus The Man

There are many people who hesitate to speak of the humanity of Jesus. The name Jesus was a common name in ancient Israel. It is the equivalent of the Hebrew name Joshua. Many Jewish parents chose to name their children after Joshua, the former great leader of the Israelites. Thus we are reminded that Jesus was a historical person. Yet, like the Docetists in ancient Christianity, we are sometimes uncomfortable describing Jesus as a man like others. The Docetists of the second and third centuries would not even admit that Jesus came in the flesh. They wanted to preserve His distance from the rest of us. Many Christians have followed the lead of the Docetists in denying that Jesus agonized through some of our common struggles. Did he really have to make difficult decisions in choosing His way? Did he ever face the same discouragements which turn our Christian service into a long, difficult road?

The author of Hebrews did not share our reticence in discussing Jesus the man. He knew that we do not really know Jesus unless we know him as a man. We may think of Jesus as some kind of angelic being who is only partially man. But this view is unacceptable in Hebrews. Immediately after he tells us that Jesus is greater than angels (Heb. 1), the author quotes the eighth psalm in chapter 2 to make the opposite point. The eighth psalm makes a beautiful statement about man's place in the creation, but it also refers to the ideal man, Jesus Christ. The author's version of the Old Testament (the Septuagint) says that he was made "a little while lower than the angels." So while chapter 1 says the Son is "better than angels" (1:4), chapter 2 says he was "a little while lower than angels." Thus to know Jesus is not only to know his majesty, it is to know of his abasement below the angels "for a little while." This was the period of Jesus' life on earth.

Before the crown there was the cross (Heb. 2:10). Before his glory he was "made lower" than the angels. The New Testament affirms this message many times. Paul writes that God has highly exalted the One who "emptied himself" (Phil. 2:7). We are told also here that the One who is now

30

crowned was once "made lower than the angels." We do not know Jesus until we learn that the suffering of death preceded his reign. Christianity is the religion of a man who suffered and died, a man whose presence was recorded by historians. We maintain our proper direction only as long as we remain rooted in the story of that man.

We should not consider this discussion of Jesus' humanity as irrelevant speculation. It says something very important to a community that has suffered the trials of the long march. Many of the readers suffered imprisonment and loss of property (10:32ff.). No doubt many others wondered if there was any end in sight to their struggle for the cause of Christ. Perhaps they wondered if they were suffering for a lost cause. Consequently, the words about the humanity of Jesus are very important. They tell us that we are not suffering alone. As Hebrews 2:10 says, we have a "pioneer of our salvation."

The Pioneer And Hero

The word for "pioneer" (*archēgos*) is used in only one book besides Hebrews (Acts 3:15, 5:31). It was the common Greek word for a hero who founded a city and gave it his name. In other instances, it was used for the head of a clan, or the progenitor of a people, as Abraham was the progenitor of the Jews. Basically, the word means "originator." The New English Bible renders it "leader." The idea of the "forerunner" (*prodromos*) in 6:20 is closely related. The word "pioneer" also describes Jesus in Hebrews 12:2. The idea suggests that Christ is the "trailblazer" who first made the pilgrimage that we now are making. As Hebrews 10:20 says, he "opened up the new and living way."

31

The author reminds us in 12:2 that Christ is the "pioneer and perfector of our faith." He walked in our place and experienced our pain, but now he has opened the way to God. His example encourages us to follow.

To people who are tired of the journey, it is encouraging to know that the long road has been conquered by someone ahead of us. For this reason, it is essential that we know Jesus. To recognize him as our pioneer is to recognize that the promised land lies beyond our momentary frustrations. He has not asked us to face any struggles which he has not faced himself.

"To people who are tired of the journey, it is encouraging to know that the long road has been conquered by someone ahead of us."

We would not find much comfort if our pioneer had not really faced our difficulties. Indeed, the inspiration which a pioneer provides comes from the fact that he has faced crises like our own. We look back, for instance, at American heroes with admiration because they endured conditions at least as difficult as our own. In the same way, our pioneer is of the same nature as those who follow. "For he who sanctifies and those who are sanctified have all one origin" (Heb. 2:11). Jesus is not the remote and unmoved deity whom the Greeks worshipped. He identifies with us. He calls us his brothers (Heb. 2:12). As a man like us, he too was faced with trusting God along the way to the promised land (Heb. 2:13). Indeed, he is our one great model of faith.

As active people never satisfied with maintaining

the status quo, Americans appreciate the image of the pioneer. We depend on them to open new territories and to introduce technological advances that keep us moving. Some of these achievements came at great human cost, and we are indebted to those who opened the way. Alistair Cook described the incredible adventure of Charles Lindbergh in his book, *America*. In 1927 Lindbergh landed in Paris after a flight which had taken thirty-three hours. For sheer daring, this flight was as spectacular as the moon landing. Lindbergh had survived without communication with anyone. If his mission had failed midway through the course, there were no contingency plans to rescue him. He had literally pioneered a new era, and many others later followed his model.

Jesus is a model for us because he is a brother to us and was subjected to our limitations. He is our pioneer in suffering and glory. We do not know him unless we take his humanity seriously.

There is always a temptation, especially after the death of a great man, to glorify him so much that we deify him. Ancient literature emphasizes the divine-like qualities of Augustus Caesar and Alexander the Great to show that they were not ordinary men. Indeed, the emperors expected to receive honors due their gods. Even many Jewish writings exalted past biblical heroes to emphasize their divinelike qualities. For instance, a story in the noncanonical book known as Enoch quotes Noah's father as saying: "I have a remarkable son who is not like other men, for he is like the sons of God in the heavens . . . He is not as we are; his eyes are like rays of the sun and his countenance is majestic" (Eth. Enoch 106:5).

"In Every Respect"

The author says in Hebrews 2:14, "Since therefore the children share in flesh and blood, he himself partook of the same nature." As sons of the same father, Christ and men are brothers, and brothers share the same nature. In this passage the author uses two words which vividly describe Jesus' humanity. It is said, for instance, that children "share flesh and blood." The word for "share" (*koinōneō*) means to "have in common." All men and women share human limitations that go with flesh and blood. Then, says the author, he "likewise partook of the same nature." The word for "partake" (*metechō*) is a synonym for "share." We learn that the humanity of Christ was genuine. He shared everything involved with being made of flesh and blood.

No writer of the New Testament affirms the humanity of Jesus like the author of Hebrews. He says in 2:17, "He had to be made like his brethren in every respect." The Greek word for "made like" (*homoiōthēnai*) suggests not merely similarity. It suggests an identical nature. The words "in every respect" indicate that there is no exception to Jesus' full identification with mankind. Our pioneer has stood where we stand.

A Share In Our Temptations

Do we understand what it means to say that Jesus is our brother and pioneer? For those of us struggling with temptation, it is particularly encouraging to know that our pioneer has experienced the same temptations. To say that our pioneer has stood where we now stand is to say that he knows the full power of our trials. As Hebrews says, "For because he has suffered and been

34

tempted, he is able to help those who are tempted" (2:18). And the writer stresses it in Hebrews 4:15: "For we do not have a high priest who is unable to sympathize with our weaknesses, but one who in every respect has been tempted as we are, and yet without sin."

He was anguished over the fear of death (2:14). There is never an attempt to gloss over this anguish in Gethsemane. He was fearful of death, as we are (Heb. 5:7). He uttered "loud cries and tears" to the God who could save Him from death. It is difficult for us to understand fully the temptations of Jesus. We do not understand such a life of absolute trust which did not submit to temptation. But while we may not understand, we should not forget that Jesus was a man with our temptations.

The readers of this book were especially tempted to give up. The long march, and with it the threat of persecution and pain of believing, tempted them to drop out before they had reached their goal. The end was not in sight. The Christian life had become frustrating.

According to the author, the answer for their frustration was realizing that their pioneer had known the agony, pain, and frustration of the long march himself. And yet he never quit. He completed the journey. Now that he has reached the goal, he can "sympathize" (Heb. 4:15) with us.

We also can benefit, in our frustration today, by remembering that our faith did not begin with a continuous string of victories. It began with a pioneer who was tempted to quit in the presence of adversity. And it has continued through generation after generation of Christians who discovered that the Christian life involves a test of endurance.

Someone To Depend On

We will never survive in the midst of adversity unless we discover something reliable and secure on which we can rely. The church can never live on temporary, fascinating diversions. Nor can we base our lives on ideologies which shift with the wind. Many of the securities we build our lives on are not secure. The author of Hebrews reminds us that our pioneer is "merciful and faithful" (2:17). The word for "faithful" (*pistos*) means "reliable." It is the word we use for someone whose word can be trusted. As Hebrews 10:23 says, "He who promised is faithful."

4

Striving for the Rest

"Let us therefore strive to enter that rest."

Hebrews 3:7–4:11

We traditionally have made history one of the pillars of the school curriculum. We are required to study names and dates connected with the crucial events of our history, presumably because we expect to learn important lessons to guide us today. The mere recollection of significant names from the past is supposed to suggest some important lesson which we have learned.

But we have not always learned from history. Often we repeat the same mistakes. We are tempted to resign ourselves from looking at the past, perhaps because we continue to learn the wrong lessons. Henry Ford reportedly expressed a popular view when he said, "History is bunk." Someone else once said, "The only thing we learn from history is that we do not learn from history."

Christians cannot avoid looking at the past because biblical faith is rooted in history. We are heirs of a history that extends from the first pages of the Bible until now. It is no accident that the Bible is filled with narratives intended to teach us a lesson. Whether we read the stories of Abraham and Sarah or the later narratives of the fall of Israel and Judah, we learn something about ourselves. Like the people of God in both testaments, we experience both the hopes and struggles of being faithful. Thus when we read the Bible, we discover people like ourselves who face situations like ours. As Paul Minear wrote,

> It is as if in the theater, where I am hugely enjoying an esthetic view of life, God interrupts the show with a stentorian announcement: 'Is John Smith in the House?' And I am John Smith. And the interruption continues, 'Report immediately . . . for a task intended for you alone.'[1]

People who have discovered in recent years the importance of finding their roots cannot afford to ignore their heritage in the narratives of the Bible. These narratives have already addressed many generations, and they will benefit us also if we will permit them to speak to us. We maintain our steadfast commitment by finding our roots in this story. Without it, we would drift along, subject to any new idea our culture might offer.

Why Study The Old Testament?

The world of the Old Testament seems far away from us. We wonder what the exodus story or the account of the conquest of Canaan has to say to us. Often the study of these books has involved nothing more than the repetition of obscure facts which hardly touch our Christian lives today. We read the Old Testament only to discover genealogies of important persons, or to find the prophecies to be fulfilled. Many times we find only a strange world of incidents that have little meaning for us.

For the author of Hebrews, the Old Testament was not a collection of irrelevant facts. He knew that the narratives had a message for the church in his time. The author found lessons in the Old Testament for people of his time who were growing weary and apathetic in their Christian pilgrimage.

A Pilgrimage Of Faith

There were Old Testament pilgrims who faced a situation like ours. Joshua, whose name in Hebrew was the equivalent for Jesus (Heb. 4:8 KJV) led this pilgrimage. The story of the conquest was not a happy one. It included grumbling and disobedience. The people God released from Egyptian slavery did not enjoy a constant series of triumphs. It would have made a happier story for victories of the conquest to follow immediately after victories of the exodus. But the people who left Egypt had to wait a long time before they entered the promised land—if they entered the promised land at all. Between the two victories there was a period of grumbling, disobedience, and temptation to give up on the pilgrimage. And even worse, most of the people failed to reach the promised land after a dazzling beginning. This story became a lesson for the early church. As Hebrews 4:11 says, "This story was an example to the church" (ASV, NEB).

Hebrews is not the only book of the New Testament to discover a model for the church in this wilderness episode. In 1 Corinthians, Paul wrote about Christians who apparently believed that their salvation guaranteed that they could never fall. Paul wrote about the wilderness story to these Christians, saying, "Now these things happened to them as a warning, but they were written down for our instruction" (1 Cor. 10:11). Biblical narratives reach across the centuries to speak to us. We have both good and bad models of response to God's grace. And we need to hear both. There are times when our faith is strengthened by seeing the worthy models of those who have responded in faith, as we notice in Hebrews 11. At other times, the Bible gives us examples of disobedience and failure so we might learn from their experience.

A Word Of Warning (3:7-19)

We see that Hebrews 3:7–4:11 is a sermon on the subject of the pilgrim people. Like a good preacher, the author bases his sermon entirely on scripture. The scripture quoted in Hebrews 3:7-11 is taken from Psalm 95:7-11. In the psalmist's memory of the wilderness generation, he recalls God's anger with people who had failed in the time of temptation. Even though Joshua 21:44 had said that "the Lord gave them rest on every side" (Deut. 12:9, 25:19), the psalmist recalls another side of the story—God's stern oath that "they shall never enter my rest" (Ps. 95:11, Heb. 3:11). The psalmist recalls the tragedy of those who did not reach the goal, not the victories of the conquest. They discovered God was not to be toyed with.

What do we learn from our study of the Old Testament? What does the story of the wilderness wandering say to us today? Hebrews 3:12-19 suggests that the Bible warns us. The stern words of the psalm are also addressed to us: "good news came to us just as it came to them" (4:2). We too are on the way to the promised land. We are on a journey filled with doubt and despair, a pilgrimage that is never easy. And, like the wilderness generation, we began our journey with high expectations for joy and triumph along the way. Some of those expectations turned to disappointment.

"People are often tempted to read the Bible to support or defend a position they have already taken."

We cannot miss the element of gravity that pervades Hebrews. The author consistently sees in the Old Testament a warning to people who trifle with God's invitation. He asks in 2:3, "How shall we escape if we neglect such a great salvation?" In 12:29, he says, "Our God is a consuming fire," the "one with whom we have to do" (4:13). The Old Testament presents us not only the model of heroes who lived by faith, but also negative examples like Esau who "found no place to repent" (12:17). Once the author says, "Do not refuse him who is speaking" (12:25). The Old Testament includes reminders that our salvation is conditioned by our response. "It is a terrible thing to fall into the hands of the living God." The God who pronounced a judgment on Israel also warns us.

People are often tempted to read the Bible to support or defend a position they have already taken. We like to identify with the heroes and to think of ourselves as having their virtues. But this is not the only way to read the Bible. We should also see ourselves as disobedient and rebellious

41

children of God like the murmuring children of Israel. Therefore, the author of Hebrews says, "Take care, brethren, lest there be in any of you an evil, unbelieving heart, leading you to fall away from the living God" (3:12). When the early Christians looked back on the story of disobedient Israel, they did not self-righteously conclude that they would do better. Paul concluded from this story, "Let anyone who thinks he stands take heed lest he fall" (1 Cor. 10:12). History tells us we too can fall away. We began the pilgrimage as they did. Their failure to reach the goal is a lesson for the church.

Hebrews 3:16-18 clearly states the lessons from history. The author asks five questions which dramatically confront the listeners. The first and third questions are answered by the second and fourth questions. The fifth question contains its own answer. The point is clear: those who began the pilgrimage under the mighty acts of God were the same ones who were destroyed in the wilderness. Their unbelief led to their failure (3:19).

If We Hold Fast

These questions underline the fact that our salvation is always conditional. Like the Israelites, we have enjoyed a good beginning. Now everything depends on us. Two passages in Hebrews indicate that our salvation is a conditional thing. "We are his house if we hold fast our confidence and pride in our hope" (3:6). "For we share in Christ, if only we hold our first confidence firm to the end" (3:14). These two verses suggest that we have been given a firm confidence. The word for "confidence" (*hypostasis*) in 3:14 means literally "some-

42

thing solid under your feet" or "a place to stand." The word translated "confidence" (*parrēsia*) is also used in 10:19. It carries the connotation of "boldness" or "freedom of speech." It was the right to appear boldly before a ruler. Now that God has given us this firm *confidence*, everything now depends on our response. We cannot miss the significance of "if" in 3:6 and 3:14.

"The professional minister isn't the only one who looks out for the pilgrims. It is the task of the whole church."

Undoubtedly the church has a perpetual problem of having some who fall away. One remedy suggested in Hebrews reminds us of our responsibilities for each other. "Take care . . . lest there be *in any of you* an unbelieving heart" (3:12). We are responsible for each other! "Encourage each other each day" (3:13). The professional minister isn't the only one who looks out for the pilgrims. It is the task of the whole church. We maintain the faith by travelling together. Alone we fall away; together we nurture each other along.

So, do we learn from history? We recognize that God's gift is to be taken seriously. We understand the wrath of God, which comes as a warning to any age tempted to give up on his promise. Their story could be our story (Heb. 4:11).

The Great Promise

There is another side of the story which we dare not overlook. The Bible is not only a threat to those of us who would consider denying God's gift.

43

It also encourages us when we are tempted to fail. Despite our chronic disobedience and ingratitude, God still achieves his purposes. When Israel complained earlier about the absence of God, she learned that his absence was not final. When Elijah believed he was the only faithful person left, he discovered that God still had 7,000 people who had not bowed to Baal.

Thus, in addition to the wrath of God which we learn of in the Bible, there are also words of encouragement. Many times it is encouragement which we need most to hear. Paul reminds us, "By the encouragement of the Scriptures we might have hope" (Rom. 15:4). We look to the Scriptures not only to see ourselves in Israel's failures, but also to hear God's promise to Israel and to us. The entire biblical story demonstrates that God's word of promise is trustworthy.

"The key to the survival of the church may lie in its response to frustration and disappointment."

Much of the imagery of our hymns pictures the church as pilgrim people overlooking the promised land. Hope in the future keeps us alive on the pilgrimage. We cannot remain faithful if no future awaits us. Viktor Frankl observed from his years in a Nazi prison camp that only those people who believed in a future had the will to go on in extreme adversity. Despite hunger and intense pain, even the slightest ray of hope that something awaited them outside prison gave them amazing endurance.

Israel's experience is like our own. We too stand before God's promise. The good news is that "we who have believed enter that rest" (Heb. 4:3). The promise still remains for us! But it is not the promised land of the Old Testament that we expect. Hebrews 4:4 suggests that we are now on our way to the kind of rest which only God knows, for He "rested on the seventh day." We look forward to sharing that rest with Him.

What can motivate us to continue the pilgrimage when we feel that we can go no farther? After the author of Hebrews says, "There remains a sabbath rest for the people of God" (4:9), he concludes his sermon, "Let us therefore strive to enter that rest, that no one fall by the same sort of disobedience" (4:11). The goal ahead of us provides our motivation to "break camp" and continue on our way. The experience of Israel warns us not to quit. The promise of God gives us the will to "strive to enter that rest." Both the warning and the promise motivate us.

A church that is not rooted in its past will have no resources for countering the inevitable frustrations and disappointments of the Christian life. Without our roots in the past experiences of the people of God, we are most likely to repeat their mistakes and "fall by the same sort of disobedience" (Heb. 4:11). Without our roots, we will understand neither the wrath nor the mercy of God, and thus we will be unprepared for the demands of the long pilgrimage.

The key to the survival of the church may lie in its response to frustration and disappointment. Disappointment has been a part of the life of faith from the days of Israel until now. A church that knows its history is aware of both the tragedy of failing to endure and the motivating power of God's promise.

---

[1]Paul Minear, *Eyes of Faith* (1946), p. 19.

5

Hearing God's Word

"The word of God is living and active . . ."

Hebrews 4:12-13

"For the word of God is living and active, sharper than any two edged sword, piercing to the division of soul and spirit, of joints and marrow, and discerning the thoughts and intentions of the heart. And before him no creature is hidden, but all are open and laid bare to the eyes of him with whom we have to do."

These beautiful reflections were written to a tired church. They came at a crucial point in the appeal of the author of Hebrews to his weary community. After he urged his readers to remain faithful in the midst of the temptation to drop out, he told his tired community that their greatest need is to be challenged by the word of God.

These thoughts may appear incredible to many of us who search for ways of bringing vitality to a lethargic church. The author's enthusiasm for the word of God seems to be naive to many contemporary Christians. Instead of seeing the word of God as the *answer* for a dying church, many people today suspect that it is the *cause* for much of our apathy. By the time we are adults, many of us assume that we have been innoculated with the Bible. If some people think the Bible is dull and tedious, we may have done our share to make it seem boring. There is a black cover with the words "Holy Bible" stamped in gold. Inside we find microscopic print in two parallel columns on each page. Someone has numbered each sentence—a procedure that would wreck the most exciting novel you ever read.[1]

"To renew the church, it seems more persuasive to us to examine what is happening now instead of what happened centuries in the past."

When you mention Bible study, you are likely to get some of these reactions. "I heard all of those stories by the time I was twelve." "Bible study involves memorizing trivial details that have nothing to do with my life." "It involves opening the Bible at random to see if we can find some special wisdom." "It involves looking up the appropriate passage to prove my point." It is no wonder, then, that it sounds naive for the Hebrews writer to suggest that a tired community be challenged by the word of God. For us, the Bible has become irrelevant, tedious, and boring.

We may be facing a backlash with regard to the study of the Bible. We have seen the Scripture misused so many times by people who only wanted to use it to prove a point that we have become afraid of involvement with the text. We are tempted to imply that we do not take the Bible seriously. We may develop a flippant attitude toward Bible study time. We may use this time for anything but reflection on Scripture, or we may arrange study programs on topics that are marginal in biblical content, or we may select topics that are the current fads. To renew the church, it seems more persuasive to us to examine what is happening now instead of what happened centuries in the past. The word of God is living and active—the opposite of what we have been led to believe.

Living And Active

For us, words can be cheap. We make promises to each other that we do not take seriously. We make oaths to God that we easily break. It is easy for our words to mean nothing because too often we have turned them into nothing.

But God is different. He says to Jeremiah, "Is not my word like fire . . . and like a hammer which breaks a rock in pieces" (Jer. 23:29). Our commitments may be meaningless, but God's word is lasting. "The grass withers, the flower fades; but the word of our Lord abides forever" (Isa. 40:8).

The first readers of another memorable passage in Isaiah must have asked if all of God's promises had failed. They saw no reason to continue to believe. Their land had been left desolate, and their people had given up on God. It was then that the prophet said,

> For as the rain and the snow come down
> > from heaven, making it bring forth and
> sprout,
> > and return not thither but water the
> > earth,
> > giving seed to the sower and bread
> > to the eater,
> so shall my word be that goes forth
> > from my mouth;
> > it shall not return to me empty,
> but it shall accomplish that which I
> > purpose,
> > and prosper in the thing for which I
> > sent it.

Isaiah 55:10-11

The story of the Bible concerns people who sometimes had nothing to sustain them but a promise. They often seemed on the brink of collapse. Sarah laughed at the idea of God's fulfilling His promise. Abraham must have been bewildered as he made his way up Mount Moriah to sacrifice his son Isaac. Elijah traveled to Mount Horeb certain that God's cause was lost, because he believed that he was the only one left. The Israelites wept in Babylon over the failure of God's purposes. But the promise was not extinguished. It looked that way, even at Calvary, but God brought hope out of despair. As Paul told the Corinthians, "All the promises of God find their yes in him" (2 Cor. 1:20).

A Happy Ending

The Bible is not a book of thousands of isolated verses. It concerns the God whose word is "living and active," who offers our lives a promise. The readers of Hebrews had shown signs of boredom that we have also seen in the life of the church. But the writer reminds them that it is the challenge of Scripture which stimulates and encourages. The God who once made a promise to Abraham and Moses holds out the same promise to His church today. We may share the frustrations of Elijah or Sarah, but Scripture reminds us that God's word "is living and active."

We have good reason to be disturbed since so much of our reading material and entertainment focuses on the theme of hopelessness and chaos of life. In the place of old films where beauty and truth always won, we now have a steady diet of struggle by the forces of good against hopeless odds. We vainly wish for an occasional happy ending.

In John Fowles' *Daniel Martin*, the playwright-hero reflects on his craft. "He thought, for instance, . . . how all through his writing life, both as a playwright and a scenarist, he had avoided the happy ending, as if it were somehow in bad taste." As he considered how to complete his story, it occurred to him that "it had become offensive . . . to suggest publicly that anything might turn out well in the world." Today's steady diet of novels, plays, and movies appears to reflect a similar point of view; it would be bad taste to suggest that things do turn out well.

In the Bible things do turn out well. And people who are inundated with the message of hopelessness need to be refreshed by the word of hope that comes in Scripture. A tired church needs to hear about the Bible's happy ending.

Paul's letter to the Romans speaks of the hope which Scripture provides. "For whatever was written in former days was written for our instruction, that by steadfastness and by the encouragement of the Scriptures we might have hope" (Rom. 15:4). Hopelessness and chaos do not have the last word in the Bible. That is probably why the church may be one community that has not lost its hope in a society where we are showered by words of despair. In Scripture we discover the God whose word is "living and active."

Early Christians were sustained largely by the conviction that the thread running through the Bible was the word of promise. They recalled that God had made promises to Abraham (Gen. 12:2) and David (2 Sam. 7:10-17). In the coming of Jesus Christ they recognized that God had kept his promise. Paul told his listeners in one speech, "We bring you the good news that what God promised to the fathers, this he has fulfilled to us their children by raising Jesus" (Acts 13:32-33). The good news was the word that was "promised beforehand through His prophets in the holy Scriptures" (Rom. 1:2). The Scripture was "living and active," for it demonstrated that God keeps His word.

Sharper Than Any Two-Edged Sword—Divine Surgery

The word of God is not only a word of hope. Obviously, there are times when we need words of hope more than we need anything else. But there is another aspect of Scripture. It is "sharper than any two-edged sword, piercing to the division of soul and spirit, of joints and marrow, discerning the thoughts and intentions of the heart." The imagery suggests an especially fine-cutting instrument—a two-edged sword. It pierces and cuts. The Bible is not dull or boring. It is not a weapon to be used on others. It does surgery, but not on others.

As we read the Bible, we discover that it is doing surgery on us. We are exposed and "laid open" before it. We are confronted with the "one with whom we have to do." The word for "laid open" (*tetrachēlismena*) is the term for the sacrificial animal whose neck was "laid open." We do not go to the Bible only to confirm our prejudices. The Bible is more like the surgeon's knife which exposes us or the mirror which shows our flaws when we prefer not to see them. Indeed, the Bible is our most relentless critic. We might translate the words of 4:12: "critical of the thoughts and intentions of the heart." Today's English Version of the Bible says, "It judges the thoughts and intentions of the heart."

"As we read the story of the spiritual dropouts in the wilderness, we must account for our own spiritual lives."

The letters of Paul were written precisely because people had distorted the faith and needed correction. The letters of John also were addressed to people who had misunderstood and distorted the faith. Leander Keck wrote, "We delude ourselves if we think the first readers treated each new work as a gift from heaven." The words came as criticism of their lives.

We may consider Old Testament stories as suitable only for children. But if we read them closely we notice that they are a series of critiques of the behavior of God's people. Perhaps the people wanted to have things their own way. But if their religion had been what it should have been, there would have been no need for the word of the prophet to carry out its surgery on the people.

The author of Hebrews makes it clear that the word of God is still alive, and it still carries out its surgery. As we read the story of the spiritual drop-outs in the wilderness we must account for our own spiritual lives. We are drawn into the story and warned because we are also recipients of the good news (Heb. 4:2). We might prefer merely a word of congratulations on our successful Christian lives. But we, like the original recipients of the word of the Lord, are judged and criticized by the one "with whom we have to do."

I'm OK, You're OK?

Many people in our culture do not want to be held accountable to anything. The only thing that seems to matter is to have our own needs fulfilled. We hold ourselves aloof from our commitments to our family and friends because they might inhibit our self-fulfillment. If the reigning philosophy is "I'm OK, You're OK," or "I do my thing, you do your thing," the emphasis is on a life without standards, a life with no challenges. All we want is a word to tell us that we are "OK." Henry Fairlie says in *The Seven Deadly Sins Today* that the one thing held in common by various representatives of the human potential movement is that "in spite of the apparent emphasis in some of them on self-development disciplines, the self-examination and self-correction that are demanded are paltry."

People in the church today often are tempted to allow their faith to become just one more human potential movement designed to tell us that we are

"OK." Elmer F. Suderman imagined one minister's vision of church life like this:

"Words of cheap grace do not sustain the life of the church. It is the confrontation with God's word of judgment which calls us to repentance and accountability."

Here they are
my pampered flamboyants,
status spoiled, who bring
with exquisite zing
their souls spick and span
protected by Ban,
their hearts young and gay
decked with handsome cliche,
exchanging at my call
worship for whispering
God for gossiping,
theology for television.

Baptized in the smell
of classic Chanel
I promote their nod
to a jaunty God
Who, they are sure,
is a sparkling gem
superbly right for them.

Words of cheap grace do not sustain the life of the church. It is the confrontation with God's word of judgment which calls us to repentance and accountability. We need time to examine and reflect on the words of Scripture. Without those times we subject ourselves to fads which come and go. We may forget our identity if there is no word to challenge us.

Augustine, the great theologian of the early fifth century, was torn between a Christian mother and a pagan father as a child. As a youth he experimented with various philosophies, all the while giving in to immorality and dissipation. But finally, after years of experimentation, he gave up his old ways to become a Christian. He said a great turning point in his life came when he heard the reading of Romans 13:12ff.: "The night is far gone, the day is at hand. Let us then cast off the works of darkness and put on the armor of light; let us conduct ourselves becomingly as in the day, not in reveling and drunkenness, not in debauchery and licentiousness, not in quarreling and jealousy. But put on the Lord Jesus Christ, and make no provision for the flesh, to gratify its desires." It was as if those words had been addressed to him. They challenged his life and called him to repent.

Today God's word still works its surgery. And unless we submit ourselves to the surgery of God's word, the church will cease to be His church.

---

[1]David H.C. Read, *Overheard* (New York and Nashville: Abingdon Press, 1969).

6

Developing Christian Maturity

"By this time you ought to be teachers"

Hebrews 5:-6:12

In the Middle Ages, a list was made of the "seven deadly sins." The authors must have considered these seven sins worse than any others. The "seven deadly sins" contained such expected things as pride, envy, anger, avarice, gluttony, and lust. But there is one surprising item—the word *accidie*, which is normally translated "laziness" or "sloth." We may not think of it as one of our most serious offenses because to us the word "sin" normally conjures up images of sexual or anti-social offenses. But the ancient church considered "sloth" to be one of its most serious offenses.

Another characteristic of *accidie* might be a "couldn't-care-less" attitude. We might think that our problems are very different from those of ancient people because our lives are more complicated than theirs. But listen to this description of a lazy fifth-century monk:

> When the poor fellow is beset by it, it makes him detest the place where he is, and loathe his cell; and he has a poor and scornful opinion of his brethren, near and far, and thinks that they are neglectful and unspiritual. It makes him sluggish and inert for every task; he cannot sit still, nor give his mind to reading; he thinks despondently how little progress he has made where he is, how little good he gains or does . . . he dwells on the excellence of other and distant monasteries; he thinks how profitable and healthy life is there; how delightful the brethren are, and how spiritually they talk. On the contrary, where he is, all seems harsh and untoward; there is no refreshment for his soul to be got from his brethren, and none for his body from the thankless land ; . . . and so, with his mind full of stupid bewilderment and shameful gloom, he grows slack and void of all spiritual energy, and thinks that nothing will do him any good save to go and call on somebody, or else to betake himself to the solace of sleep.[1]

Sloth is also our problem. We see the debilitating effects of not caring. Discouragement easily robs us of our will to go on with our Christian calling.

The Hebrews author says in 6:12, "That you may not be sluggish . . . ." One of their main problems was that they had "drooping hands and weak knees." Having lost their original intensity, they were vulnerable to new ideas or doctrines (13:9). This sluggishness was especially evident in the problem of lack of church attendance (10:25) and in their temptation to "neglect" their great salvation. Sluggishness was only the beginning of what could turn into apostasy (6:6).

Dull Of Hearing

There is more than one way to be sluggish. We have already noticed some of the symptoms of sluggishness among the readers of Hebrews. But there is another aspect of sluggishness often overlooked. In 5:11 the author suddenly says, "You have become dull of hearing."

In 5:1-10, the author starts the central section of the book showing that Jesus Christ is the high priest after the order of Melchizedek. After describing the levitical requirements for priesthood (5:1-4), he demonstrates that Jesus Christ fulfills all requirements. Having experienced the agony of suffering (5:8-9), He has been designated the "high priest after the order of Melchizedek" (5:10). This fact is first mentioned in 5:10 and is then developed in chapters 5-10. For most people, the argument about the high priesthood of Christ is the most memorable section of the epistle. We learn that Jesus is no ordinary priest. Unlike levitical high priests, He lives forever (7:3, 23).

To our surprise, this discussion is interrupted in 5:11. The author leaves the subject to address his readers personally. We know that the author consistently ends his expositions of the Old Testament with some words of encouragement. The longest exhortation in the book is found in 5:11–6:12.

The subject which the author introduced in 5:10 is too difficult for the readers. "About this we have much that is hard to explain." The word "hard to explain" (*dusermēneutos*) literally means "hard to communicate," not "hard to interpret." Hebrews is sometimes known for its difficult arguments, especially in the description of Christ and Melchizedek. We wonder why the author pursued a matter that is "hard to explain" with Christians who were dropping out of the community. Why didn't he try "pep rallies" or other new gimmicks to stir their interest? We think the church should consider things that are "hard to explain" only after all other matters have been solved.

Or we reserve such matters for the experts, not the entire church. But the author of Hebrews was convinced that matters "hard to explain" were meant for the whole church—even a tired and bored church—to pursue, because in chapters 7-10 he continues this difficult message.

"The author of Hebrews, a model preacher, knows that a living church maintains its vitality through both exhortation and information."

We may wonder why the author pursues such a topic in a book on church renewal. The answer, undoubtedly, is that the only renewal that matters is the renewal that is lasting. There is a need for depth and roots if we are going to maintain our vitality for a long period. A pep rally may be useful for a short while. But a church that endures needs a firm anchor (Heb. 6:19) where it can find the security and encouragement to keep the faith. Archimedes, the Greek mathematician, once said, "Give me a place to stand, and I will move the world." The author of Hebrews introduced a topic "hard to explain" because he knew the church needed a place to stand.

It is easy to lose the balance between the tasks of informing and exhorting in preaching. A sermon that merely informs may never confront the audience with the demands of God on their lives. A sermon which only exhorts may easily be without substance. The author of Hebrews, a model preacher, knows that a living church maintains its vitality through both exhortation and information. He recognizes that a church needs firm roots in solid, demanding study. He is not afraid of confronting Christians with challenging words. He knows that a faith that is easily reduced to a few slogans does not give us a firm place to stand. There is a place in biblical preaching for a challenge to our minds. There is no substitute for words that are "hard to explain" because the enthusiasm for learning provides roots for living.

An Indictment

Preaching should sometimes confront us with our responsibilities and indict us for our failures. The author of Hebrews says that the word is difficult to explain because "you are dull in hearing." The word for "dull" (*nōthros*) is the same word that is translated "sluggish" in 6:12. This word was often used for a lazy student who refused to develop his mind. The author might have said, "The fault does not lie in the word itself. The fault is yours. You have not developed the capacity to understand."

The readers had apparently been Christians for at least a generation. The author mentions the amount of time which has elapsed since they first became Christians ("because of the time," 5:12). The readers had sufficient time to sharpen their minds and become competent to teach. Their problem was sluggishness manifested in lack of physical and intellectual energy.

The answer for a tired church, according to the author, is to be fed "solid food." In ancient times, a beginning philosophy student was introduced to a few "first principles" by his teacher. The student was often described as a "babe" who had to rely first on "milk" before he went on to "solid food." The students intended to develop their potential in order to become teachers themselves. Any student who remained at the beginning level for a long period of time caused serious problems.

This was appropriate imagery for the author of Hebrews. After a generation, the readers were still in their infancy (5:13). Their diet consisted of milk, and they were unable to digest the solid food that the author would offer. The author probably looked at the tired community and wanted to say something that would strengthen their faith. But he observed that their lack of intellectual growth made it almost impossible for him to communicate what they needed most. He recognized that the church can never maintain its identity unless it is grounded in the solid food of the word of God.

A Faith For Our Minds

According to the author of Hebrews, Christianity cannot survive unless it is taught. It must be treasured enough to capture our minds. Christians in every age have set up schools to pursue the scholarly study of Scripture. The health and vitality of Christianity benefits from a respect for learning. As heirs of a long, respected tradition of learning, we depend on the survival of educated church members. Faith must be explained, and faith seeks understanding. Only a very shallow, inconsequential religion makes no demands for continued learning.

T. R. Glover, a great classical scholar, once explained a major reason why Christianity was victorious in the ancient world. There were many causes competing for the people's commitment, but Christianity conquered their minds and hearts. Glover said Christians did better thinking than other people.

> The Christian read the best books, assimilated them, and lived the freest intellectual life the world had known. Jesus had set him to be free to fact.

> There is no place for an ignorant Christian. From the very start every Christian had to know and to understand, and he had to read the gospels, he had to be able to give a reason for his faith.

> They read about Jesus, and they knew him, and they knew where they stood . . . . Who did the thinking in that ancient world? Again and again it was the Christian. He out-thought the world.[2]

Perhaps Glover overstated it, but Christianity would not have survived if ancient Christians had not been able to understand and explain their faith.

A Waste Of Time?

We sometimes think of study as a waste of time or a diversion from more important things. We live in a culture which favors action over reflection. But we must question the value of actions which are not guided by careful study and reflection. The author makes a careful distinction between those who are nourished on milk and those who are nourished on meat. Those who exist on milk are "unskilled in the word of righteousness" (5:13). Those who live on meat "have their faculties trained through practice to distinguish good from evil" (5:14). The word for "unskilled" literally means "inexperienced" or "ignorant." The author says there are Christians who remain perpetually like beginning students. The "word of righteousness" or the Christian faith remains incomprehensible to them because they have no habit of careful study and reflection and no recognition that faith requires an understanding, responsive mind.

"We live in a culture which favors action over reflection."

On the other hand, there are Christians who can distinguish between good and evil because their mind has been trained by practice. Here the author uses the illustration of an athlete who trains himself through habits of practice and self-control. The same language was sometimes used for the discipline of the philosophy student because he knew the importance of training the mind.

In the same way, there is training in the Christian faith. We can develop the necessary sensitivity to make moral decisions only through this kind of training. As the author of Hebrews says, our minds are trained to "distinguish good from evil." Without this kind of training we have no way to evaluate new ideas. We may easily become prey for any new popular idea. Without disciplined training in the "word of righteousness," we cannot distinguish

64

between the Christian faith and the many other claims.

But Christianity is not a religion only for elite, learned people. On the contrary, there were people among the early Christians whom Paul could describe as being "not many wise, not many mighty, not many of noble birth" (1 Cor. 1:26). But Christianity called all of these people to use their own gifts to become more intelligent in the faith.

We notice also that it is not just a certain group of experts in Hebrews who were called to develop their understanding of the faith. The words "you are dull of hearing" were addressed to the whole congregation. It was the author's reminder that, while we may want responsible leadership to guide our study, others need to use their own gifts to grow up in the faith.

I wonder what the author of Hebrews would say to congregations today. Are we "sluggish in hearing?" What has happened to families who should have a fairly thorough knowledge of the basic content of the Bible? As James Smart wrote in his book *The Strange Silence of the Bible in the Church*, there is a danger that the church will largely ignore the Bible in its educational curriculum. The indictment of a bored church long ago may also be an indictment of contemporary congregations.

All educational programs based on the Bible are not equally beneficial for the vitality of the church. We often demonstrate that we do not take the Bible seriously by the way we treat it in our programs. Even though it is usually the center of our curriculum, our use of it often does not help us grow. In some instances we abuse it by limiting our study to only a few sections of the canon. And even then, it is exploited only to prove a point reached long ago. In many other instances we treat it as if it were a collection of isolated memory verses, not a book full of life. The mere fact that we use the Bible does not mean that we will "train our faculties," as Hebrews puts it. We grow when we study with enough seriousness to be prepared to hear the whole story, not just the parts we prefer to hear. We grow also, as we listen to others and learn from their research.

We wonder why people who read a lot do not read more books on religious subjects. There are some people who take their Christianity very seriously. They keep informed in many fields by reading the best books. But they seldom read a book about the realities of faith, about God, prayer, Christ, and the Bible. They do not read about new discoveries in the Near East and their impact on our understanding of the Bible.

Most of us have known people in the church with extraordinary competence in the academic, professional, or business world. But they have not grown beyond a few fundamentals in the Christian faith. In business, they have shown their keen minds and capacity for growth. They have gained the respect of others who admire their excellent knowledge of their field. But they exhibit an unbelievable immaturity when it comes to faith, because their knowledge hardly extends beyond a few well-worn slogans. The author of Hebrews is not indifferent toward the growth in our understanding. He knows sluggish minds do not give vitality to the church.

A Word Of Encouragement

The Preacher's indictment of his community is not the end of the sermon. Preaching also offers words of hope and encouragement. People must see a reason to engage in the action to which they are called. So the author of Hebrews encourages his community to leave the "elementary doctrines of Christ and go on to maturity" (6:1f). It was time for them to grow beyond the few items which they learned at the beginning. In this word of exhortation there is a stern warning that appears in two other instances of Hebrews (10:26f., 12:17). The writer says if those who have been "once enlightened" fall away, it is impossible to restore them to repentance. The author does not elaborate on his statement, so his warning is hard for us to understand. But we must remember that his words are not addressed to people who have already fallen away and are seeking readmission to the church. His major point is that our faith is far too precious to throw away. Our "enlightenment," or our beginning Christian life, only happens once. To think that we can "fall away" and then return cheapens our salvation. We must "go on to perfection." Without that progress we will die.

The preacher must also provide the resources that will challenge the people to go on. The author offers two reasons to his community to keep their commitment. First, verses 7-8 provide an illustration from nature. The land which receives rain and bears useful fruit is blessed by God. If it bears only thorns and thistles, it will be burned. God calls the land to be responsible. He provides His blessing only if the land does its part. It is the same way with this tired community. God promises His blessing only to those people who discipline themselves to grow up in the faith.

Second, we have invested so much of ourselves in the faith that it would be a tragedy to throw it away. The readers of this epistle demonstrated their "earnestness" (*spoudē*) long ago when they served the saints. In 10:32-35 there is another reminder of what their faith had meant to them. They endured loss of property and abuse from their society. They visited prisoners (10:34), endured a hard struggle (10:32), and ministered to the saints (6:10). This faith meant far too much to them to be neglected or thrown away now.

Our church life often appears unpleasant. Disagreements with others and dissatisfaction with the direction of the church can cause us to become disheartened and sluggish. We need to remember our previous investment in a cause in which we believed. If God does not forget our "work and labor of love for his sake" (6:10), our past should also stimulate us to "show the same earnestness in realizing the full assurance of hope until the end" (6:11).

If the author of Hebrews had written his book 2,000 years later, he probably would have said about the same thing. A weary church in the twentieth century needs to hear both his word of indictment (5:11-14) and his word of encouragement (6:1-11). Both sound as if they were addressed to us.

---

[1]David H. C. Read, *Virginia Woolf Meets Charlie Brown*. (Grand Rapids: Wm. B. Eerdmans, 1968) p. 141.
[2]Donald Baillie, *To Whom Shall We Go?* (New York: Scribner's Press, 1955), p. 63.

7

Waiting on the Promise

"We have this as a sure and steadfast anchor of the soul."

Hebrews 6:13–7:28

The most tragic words in the Bible may be the words of the men Jesus met on the road to Emmaus (Luke 24:13-24). As these men began to tell Jesus about recent events in Jerusalem, it was apparent that their world had been crushed. In despair one man said, "We had hoped that he was the one to redeem Israel" (Luke 24:21). Those words are among the most poignant in the Bible because they portray men who have lost their dreams. To rob people of their hope takes away their reason for going on. If these men had not heard the good news of the resurrection, their next step would have been to give up and resolve not to dream again.

The author of Hebrews knew that a tired church cannot live without hope. To say, "We had hoped," as did the men on the road to Emmaus, is to admit defeat. A weary church will not survive if it believes it works for a lost cause. Consequently, Hebrews is filled with words about hope and promise. Earlier the author said, "Therefore, while the promise of entering his rest remains, let us fear lest any of you be judged to have failed to reach it" (4:1). Later he describes the new covenant which is "enacted on better promises" (8:6). He summons his people to hold on, saying, "For you have need of endurance, so that . . . you may receive what is promised" (10:36). "For God who promised is faithful" (10:23). When the author describes past heroes of faith, he recalls that they were distinguished by their belief in the promise. Abraham and Sarah (Heb. 11:8-11) and many others (11:32-33) believed in the promise.

This truth is obvious in many ways in our daily life. A child may begin counting the days until Christmas on the day after Christmas. Many of us are willing to do work that is unpleasant if we see some reward at the end. Hours spent in study or in training become meaningful if they lead to the fulfillment of our ambitions. Years spent working for a cause are worthwhile if there is triumph at the end. Political reformers, revolutionaries, social workers, and many others recognize this fact.

A line in a poem by Alfred Lord Tennyson quotes a hospital nurse as she looks at the physical wreckage around her. "How could I serve in the wards if the hope of the world were a lie?" Her faith in the future provided her motivation for continuing. She could not believe that her work was all for nothing.

A popular song turns it around and puts it this way:

> If that's all there is, then let's keep
>   on dancing . . .
> If that's all there is, let's break out
>   the booze and have us a ball.

Judging from popular literature and songs, hope seems to be in very short supply. We live on a steady diet of news that casts doubt on our ability to maintain life on this planet. Movies and plays often reflect the hopelessness which many people experience.

It was not too different in ancient times. The Gentile Christians of Ephesians were reminded that before they became Christians they were "without hope and without God" (Eph. 2:12). The church was the one place where they might find hope and optimism to motivate them to act. Paul reflects on the resurrection in 1 Corinthians 15:58, "Therefore, be steadfast, unmovable, always abounding in the work of the Lord, knowing that your labor is not in vain." The resurrection brought hope into hopeless lives.

The book of Hebrews resonates with hope because weary people need to know that their pilgrimage is directed toward a goal. We can learn much from Hebrews. We learn with the original readers to give up false hopes which turn out to be mirages. We reaffirm the one hope that nourishes our lives and motivates us to keep the faith.

Life Founded On The Promise (6:13-20)

One puzzling fact about Hebrews is that this book alone is fascinated with the obscure Old Testament figure Melchizedek. He appears only twice in the Old Testament (Gen. 14:17-20, Ps. 110:4). Earlier in Hebrews we saw that the theme of Christ as the great high priest is extremely important (2:17, 4:14, 5:1-10). The mere mention of Melchizedek in 5:10 led to an indictment of the church's inability to understand such mature teaching (5:11–6:12). The author returns to the Melchizedek theme and develops it in 7:1–10:39. Why did the author insist on providing this unique exposition to his tired audience? Apparently this mature teaching was a matter of life and death for them.

Remember that the last words of the exhortation in 5:11–6:12 appeal to the church "that you may not be sluggish, but imitators of those who through faith inherit the promise" (6:12). The remedy for sluggishness is to recall the promises of God which were delivered in the past. Hebrews 3:4–4:11 shows bad examples of people who failed because they gave up on the future. But Hebrews 11 shows examples of faithful people whose commitment to a promise was a source of inspiration (11:9, 13, 17, 33). Melchizedek is important because his story concerns a promise which God gave long ago.

No one is more worthy of imitation than Abraham (6:13-17), to whom "God made a promise." No book of the New Testament emphasizes the promise of God as thoroughly as Hebrews does. We read about the "sabbath rest" of the future (4:9). We read of the heavenly city that awaits us (11:10, 16; 12:22; 13:14) and the reward (10:35, 11:26) that is left for the faithful. The people of God are not involved in a lost cause. The promise awakens us from our sluggishess.

One reason many people become discouraged is

that they expect instant fulfillment of all their hopes. We want our hopes fulfilled now! For those who believe that faith consists of nothing but easy victories, the first sign of frustration is a catastrophe.

Finding A Model

We learn much from a great model of faith like Abraham. We are told that Abraham, "having patiently endured, obtained the promise" (6:15). There were no easy victories. The story of Abraham in Hebrews 6:14 refers to the aftermath of one of the most critical struggles in Abraham's life (Gen. 22). God had commanded Abraham to offer the very child who had been promised. The commandment made no sense to Abraham, but he willingly made the effort to comply. God rescued Isaac from being sacrificed only after Abraham had shown his willingness to comply. God repeated the promise found in Hebrews 6:14 (Gen. 22:17).

Abraham was a model of faith. He obtained the promise only after a struggle. The word "patiently endured" (*makrothumeō*) is the verb form of the word "patience" in 6:12. The verb might be translated "wait patiently." It suggests a period of waiting and struggle. The struggle preceded the obtaining of the promise.

"The promise of more provides us with the patience to wait with Abraham and others."

The Bible frequently suggests that waiting is a part of the life of faith. No one likes the idea of waiting. We want constant evidence of the victory of faith. Like a child, we want instant satisfaction of our wishes. But one of the most characteristic words of the Bible is "wait." The psalms are full of this exhortation to wait. "Be still before the Lord, and wait patiently for him" (Ps. 37:7). We learn from Psalm 130:5-6

I wait for the Lord, my soul waits,
and in his word I hope;
my soul waits for the Lord
more than watchmen for the morning.

A mature church needs to learn from the models of the past. We are not the first people who have experienced frustration over the fulfillment of God's promises. If waiting is the one part of the Christian life which we do not expect, we should recall that we share the frustration and the waiting with the people of God in the past.

Someone has said that we are all in the middle of a play that began long ago when the promise was made to Abraham. Through a series of acts it has now come down to us. But there is more to come. The promise of more provides us with the patience to wait with Abraham and others.

Why We Can Wait

We may not like waiting. There may be some lingering doubt about the future if our lives are not constantly filled with victories. But we wait because God has guaranteed the future. The author makes this point in Hebrews 6:13–7:28. And, as we shall see, it is the reason he will not forget Melchizedek.

We live with more than our share of disappointments and meaningless promises. Dreams of world peace have shattered. Hopes for the eradication of poverty were premature. But God's promise is different. A striking fact about the story of Abraham

74

(Heb. 6:13-18) is the insistence on the absolute reliability of God. The story is packed with words which suggest the certainty that goes with God's promise. We are told, for instance, that God's promise to Abraham was accompanied by His solemn oath. "He swore by himself" (Heb. 6:13, Gen. 22:16). The purpose of an oath is to provide "confirmation" (Heb. 6:16). The word for "confirmation" (*bebaiōsis*) is a favorite term in Hebrews (3:6, 14; 6:19; 9:17) for something that is absolutely firm. It was the Greek word for something that was reliable or legally valid. God's oath served as his "guarantee," for he "interposed with an oath" (6:17). The word "interposed" (*mesiteuō*) literally means "to act as guarantor." We notice also that the story of God's promise in 6:13-20 emphasizes more than once the absolute "unchangeability" of the plan of God (6:17-18). Human promises may be worthless, but God's promise is unchangeable and valid.

"We are the heirs of the promise, and we find 'strong encouragement' in God's reliable word."

Now if we are in the middle of a play which began with Abraham, we need to know about the validity of God's promise. If the promise is not reliable, we have no security for times of frustration. But, according to Hebrews, it was not only for Abraham's sake that God guaranteed his promise. He wanted to "show more convincingly to the heirs of the promise the unchangeable character of his purpose" (6:17). If we are to keep the faith, we need something reliable and firm to which we can

75

hold. We are the heirs of the promise, and we find "strong encouragement" in God's reliable word (6:18).

According to Hebrews 6:18, the church, like a band of pilgrims who have "fled for refuge," needs something to grasp (the RSV translated the vivid word *krateō* "seize"). The church has found hope in God's promise which is a "sure and steadfast anchor of the soul." The imagery is powerful. People who have "fled for refuge" have no security. Without an anchor the church would drift like a ship to its destruction. The image of the anchor, which is used nowhere else in the Bible, suggests that the persecution and frustration of the Christian life can never take away from the Christian's security. The anchor enables the Christian to resist the hostile forces and hold on to something substantial.

Ancient people knew that "hope is the anchor of the soul." It gave them security. Yet hope remained in short supply. The good news of Hebrews is that this anchor was set before us when Jesus became our forerunner and "the high priest after the order of Melchizedek." Jesus opened the way for us and showed us that the future is securely ours. By entering the heavenly world and becoming the high priest after the order of Melchizedek, He gave us a future.

Eduard Schweizer, a well-known biblical scholar, compared the work of Christ to a memorable experience in his own childhood in Switzerland. His father would walk ahead in the alpine snows making footsteps for the child to follow. He showed the way for his small child. Christ has showed us the way by becoming our high priest.

We finally realize why the subject of the high priesthood of Christ, which was interrupted in 5:10, is resumed with such conviction in Hebrews 7:1–10:18. It was not a matter of idle speculation. It was a matter of life and death because the community needed to anchor its faith during a moment of frustration. Jesus Christ is God's guarantee of the future. He motivates us to endure the frustrations of the present with the knowledge that our cause is not lost.

During the early 1930s, American journalist Lincoln Steffens visited the Soviet Union and enthusiastically returned from the experiment in socialism. "I have seen the future and it works," he proclaimed. Little did he know that those words were spoken during the height of Stalin's reign of terror. Perhaps such broken promises of the past explain why hope is in short supply today. We have too often been disappointed by promises which meant nothing.

The contemporary church can learn from the words of Hebrews. The church finds its resources for living in the hope that began in Abraham and was reaffirmed in Jesus Christ.

The Order Of Melchizedek (7:1-28)

Chapter seven explains why we have a special cause for security in having a "high priest after the order of Melchizedek." This chapter explains the two verses of the Old Testament which mentioned Melchizedek. This "order" of priesthood is superior to the order of priests who served in the temple. The author exclaims, "See how great he is!" His greatness consists in the fact he has no beginning or end. He "continues a priest forever"

(7:3). The levitical priests died, but he lives (7:8). His particular order depends, not on bodily descent, but on an indestructible life (7:16). Death prevents the old order of priesthood from continuing in office, but the new order "continues for ever" (7:23-24).

As we read through chapter seven, the argument may appear difficult to understand. But the point that stands out is that the "order of Melchizedek" is eternal (7:3, 8, 16, 23-24). Jesus Christ was not qualified to be a priest of the temple (7:14), but he belongs to a priesthood that lasts forever.

The point of this chapter is that the church has not been left alone. There is one who is able "for all time" to save those who draw near, since he "always lives to make intercession for them" (7:26). A church rooted in a temporary movement has no staying power. But a church rooted in Christ, who saves "for all time," is anchored in eternity. This church will survive. We need today to reaffirm the promises which serve as an "anchor of the soul."

8

Holding on to the Prize

"Let us hold fast the confession of our hope without wavering . . ."

Hebrews 8:1–10:39

When a church shows signs of sluggishness, it needs clear words of exhortation. It needs clear words of authority and a reminder of its obligation to pursue what it has already begun. We should not be surprised to find frequent, urgent demands in Hebrews 10:19-39. "Let us draw near . . . Let us hold fast . . . without wavering; . . . and let us consider how to stir up one another to love and good works, not neglecting to meet together . . . ." The sermon must confront us with our failures and remind us of a duty to be done.

The demands of the author in verses 22, 23, 25, and 35 are spoken to a people who "have need of endurance" (10:36). They are in danger of "shrinking back" (10:39). An apathetic church needs to hear more than just the good news of God's works. It needs to hear about God's demands for "holding fast" (10:23), for good works, and for participation in the life of the church.

This is not the first section of Hebrews that calls us to be responsible. We have already seen words of appeal in Hebrews (2:1-4; 3:6, 14; 5:11–6:9). This book on renewal has accused (5:11-14), warned (2:1-4), and appealed (6:11) to the readers to maintain their commitment. One of the characteristic ways in which the author addresses his readers is with the words, "Let us . . ." (4:1, 14, 16; 6:1; 12:28; 13:13). A sluggish church has to be confronted with its responsibility.

"A church can never survive on a barrage of demands alone."

But words of appeal are never enough. A church can never survive on a barrage of demands alone. The demands mean nothing if we do not realize that we possess a gift worth preserving. Consequently, exhortation must always be accompanied with reminders of what the church has been given. This pattern is apparent in Hebrews, especially in 10:19-39. Encouragement always follows great affirmations about Jesus Christ. Thus the exhortation in 2:1-4 is based on the affirmation of chapter 1; the exhortation of 4:16 is based on God's gift which is mentioned in 4:14-15. In the same way, the exhortation in 10:19-39 comes at the end of a major section of Hebrews which began in chapter 5. The appeal is based on the account of Jesus as the great high priest.

Faith with no firm roots in God is not worth keeping. Thus before the author begins his demands ("let us . . . let us. . . let us . . .") in 10:22, he summarizes, "Since we have confidence to enter the sanctuary by the blood of Jesus . . ." (10:19). These words summarize what was said in 8:1–10:18. The references to the sanctuary, the blood of Jesus, and the "great high priest over the house of God" take us back to these chapters. Neither great affirmations nor demands can stand alone. The demand is based on the great work of Jesus Christ. What we "have" in 10:19 is our motivation for action. We may notice the author's regular reminders of what we "have" in Jesus Christ (4:14-15; 6:9; 8:1; 10:34; 13:10). That is, we have in Jesus Christ something too good to throw away.

Too Good To Throw Away

What will motivate us to remain faithful in the life of the church? Hebrews 10:19-21 mentions several items which are too important to throw away. There is, for instance, the fact that we have "confidence to enter the sanctuary" (10:19). This reminder refers to 8:1-6 where we learned that the high priestly work of Christ was done in the "true tent which is set up not by man but by the Lord" (8:2). The high priests of the Old Testament went into the tabernacle each year to carry on their obligation (Lev. 16). But their work was done in an earthly sanctuary. Hebrews 8:5 says the old sanctuary was only a "copy and shadow" of the real sanctuary. Consequently, it was inadequate, a fact which the Old Testament recognized (Heb. 8:7).

Many interpreters believe the main point of Hebrews is the statement in 8:1. The author says,

"The point in what we are saying is this: we have a high priest, one who is seated at the right hand of the majesty in heaven." The Lord whom we worship is not limited by space and time. Other leaders are finite and temporary. But the Christian stands on solid ground, knowing that his Lord is not just a person who lived in the past. Our Lord's work could not be stopped. He was exalted to God's right hand in the "real sanctuary." When we speak of Jesus as the one who was exalted to God's right hand, we acknowledge that no one else has a status like his.

The author affirms more often than any other New Testament writer that Jesus is at the right hand of God (1:3, 13; 8:1; 10:12). There is a practical reason for this insistence. Weary readers doubted if their Christian pilgrimage was worthwhile because no goal was in sight. Thus the author stresses that Jesus has opened up the way and made the goal available. Earlier Jesus was described as the "pioneer" (2:10) and "forerunner" (6:20) who blazes the trail to the goal. In 10:19 the writer says, "We have confidence to enter the sanctuary by the blood of Jesus." Consequently Jesus isn't the only one to appear before God in the sanctuary. According to 10:19, we may now enter with him.

The good news, according to Hebrews, is that Jesus has done for us what neither we nor anyone else could have done. He gave us access to God. According to 10:19, He gave us "confidence to enter." The word for "confidence" in 4:16 and 10:35 does not describe a subjective feeling. It is the word for the authority or right to approach someone of high rank. Our "right" to approach God did not exist before the work of Christ. But He "opened for us" the "new and living way." The illustration suggests an entry hall leading to the sanctuary which was closed, but now has been opened. The word for "opened" (*egkainizō*) was normally used for the dedication of a new road or building. The way to God has been opened through the death of Christ. Without Him we would have no right to come before God.

The Great Sacrifice (8:8–10:18)

Hebrews 10:19 emphasizes that what Christ has done for us we could not have done for ourselves. Our access to God came "by the blood of Jesus" (10:19) and "through his flesh" (10:20). This refers to the emphasis on sacrifice earlier in Hebrews. In 8:8-13, for instance, the author compared the two covenants and said that in the new covenant God will "remember their sins no more" (8:12). The covenant of Jesus Christ, far better than any other, releases us from our sins.

Chapter 9 includes a detailed account of the sacrifices of the old covenant. In the first covenant, sacrifices were annually offered for the sins of the people. The high priest took the blood of bulls and goats (9:7, 12-13) and made an offering "for himself and for the errors of the people" (9:7). There was no remission of sins without the shedding of blood (9:22). But those priests and their sacrifices were not really adequate (7:11). They did not succeed in purifying the conscience (9:14, 10:1). And their repeated offering suggests that they were not really effective (10:1-4). They only succeeded in reminding people of their sins (1:3). God is not satisfied with sacrifices and burnt offerings (10:8). No human activities could provide a release from guilt.

From this background, we are overwhelmed by the work of Christ. Instead of offering an ineffective sacrifice, He offered his own blood (9:11-14). Unlike the old sacrifices, his life and death did not need repeating (10:1-4; 10:11-18). At death he totally surrendered himself to the will of God (10:8-10). By that perfect obedience to the will of the Father, Christ did for humanity what it could not do for itself. He gave the perfect obedience. By giving himself, he made it possible for us to give ourselves.

"Our conscience was cleansed, not by our achievements, but by his perfect obedience."

Christians in danger of "shrinking back" (10:39) need to recognize what has been done for them. It might motivate them to endure. In Hebrews, the knowledge that Christ has done the perfect work of a high priest (8:1–10:21) provides the background for the exhortation, "Let us draw near with a true heart in full assurance of faith, with our hearts sprinkled clean from an evil conscience and our bodies washed with pure water" (10:22). We "draw near" because Christ opened the way (10:19, 6:20). Our conscience was cleansed, not by our achievements, but by his perfect obedience. We have been cleansed because at baptism His cleansing work was offered to us. It is as if we were told, "Christ gave you a new start and opened the way. It is your obligation to draw near." His sacrifice made available whatever "full assurance of faith" (v. 22) we have.

For many of us, the idea of sacrifice is difficult to understand because we have never seen an animal sacrifice. We wonder if Hebrews 8-10 communicates anything to modern readers faced with problems of a different era. While the argument may sound strange to us, we must hear the message that Christ released us from the burden of a bad conscience (10:22). Even in our secularized society, we know about the problem of a bad conscience.

Thomas Harris wrote in *I'm OK—You're OK* that we all feel, by the time we reach our adult years, that we are not "OK." A particular offense may not disturb our conscience. We just may be aware that we are not all that we should be—as neighbors, parents, husbands, and wives. Because we believe we are not "OK," we turn to the "high priests" of our society to make us whole. Today's high priest may be the therapist to whom we turn for understanding and guidance. He may be a favorite author or opinion maker. Like the readers of Hebrews, we understand what it means to have an "evil conscience" (Heb. 10:22).

"The renewal of the church cannot happen without people who are motivated by God's gift to 'stir up' others."

The New Testament, especially Hebrews, proclaims that Jesus Christ, not the other high priests, cleanses the conscience and opens the way to God. According to Hebrews 4:15, Christ is the sympathetic one who releases us from the burden of the past. When you recognize that only He cleanses the conscience, you can go on.

There is an urgent message in the exhortations of verses 23-25. We recognize the problems of a sluggish congregation. Enthusiasm and active participation in the life of the church have declined. But these demands summon the congregation to respond to God's gift. Because He has opened up the way, we now respond in the following ways. First, there is the demand to "hold fast the confession of hope without wavering." These weary Christians have been told repeatedly to "hold fast" (3:6, 14; Greek *katechō* or "seize" in 6:18) what they have been given. It is as if the author had said, "Do you recall your original confession at baptism and the good news which you have accepted? You must now hold on to what has been made available. In fact, because God is "faithful" (*pistos*, "reliable"), you now have a possession you may hold on to *without wavering*." If God is reliable, we are also to be reliable or "unwavering."

Also, the fact that we have been given a precious gift leads us to "consider how to stir up one another with love and good works" (10:24). Because of Christ we turn our attention to an enthusiasm for the community of Christians. We have a responsibility to stimulate others to action. The word in the Revised Standard Version for "stir up" in Greek is *paroxysmos*, from which we get the word "paroxysm." The word suggests our responsibility to provoke or "stir up" the community. In a very real sense, the enthusiasm of the church depends on our being agents for provoking others. The renewal of the church cannot happen without people who are motivated by God's gift to "stir up" others.

Much of the "stirring up" takes place when we meet together in worship (10:25). Undoubtedly one of the signs of the decline of the community to which Hebrews was written was the smaller attendance at worship. Perhaps some had learned a "habit" of neglecting the assembly because of a lack of interest. But no church can recapture its enthusiasm without taking public worship seriously. These meetings are the occasions for "encouraging one another."

We should be concerned about the vitality of any congregation which takes public worship lightly. Religion cannot be reduced to the mechanical repetition of certain activities, as some have done. Obviously, Christians do good works outside these assemblies. But we cannot deny that the health and vitality of the church is reflected in the collective attitude toward church attendance. Here we "stir up" and encourage one another.

Falling Into The Hands Of The Living God

The sluggishness of a community means that we take for granted God's great gift in Jesus Christ. Words describing God's gifts begin to mean nothing to us when they are so familiar that they are like an old song. Thus we read without enthusiasm that "we have become partakers of a heavenly calling" (3:1) or that we "have confidence to enter the sanctuary by the blood of Jesus" (10:19). We take for granted these gifts and become bored with them. Like one great German writer, we may only say, "God will forgive me; that is His business."

Because Christians easily take these words of God's grace for granted, there is a place for a word of warning. Hebrews tells the good news of the sacrifice of Christ, and it also warns us that we cannot trifle with God. The author asks, "How shall we escape if we neglect such a great salvation?" (2:3).

In 10:26-31 the author again warns his readers to discourage them from apostasy. This passage is one of three ominous warnings in the epistle about the impossibility of repentance for those who commit apostasy (6:4-6, 12:16-17). These words are undoubtedly among the most difficult in Hebrews for us to understand. Interpreters disagree on this passage. But while there is disagreement among scholars about the full meaning of the words, this much is certain: we are told that we cannot trifle with God. "It is a fearful thing to fall into the hands of the living God." Or, as the author says later, "Our God is a consuming fire" (12:29). We cannot fall away assuming that "God will forgive; that is his business." Jesus Christ was crucified only once. At our conversion we received the benefits of his sacrifice. If we deliberately fall away, "there remains no other sacrifice" (10:26).

Why these stern words? The author knows what it means to "fall away." He has told us about the precious gifts of Jesus Christ, gifts which consist of new life and hope. To throw all of this away would be to "recrucify the Son of God" (6:6). In 10:29 the author uses equally strong language. A deliberate apostasy would be an insult, a profaning of what is holy! It would mean "trampling" (*katapateō*) the Son of God and profaning his blood. When we recognize the greatness of the sacrifice of Christ

(Heb. 7:1–10:18), we understand why the stern warning appears in 10:26-31. Apostasy is an insult to all that God has done for us.

We must recognize that these words were not addressed to people who had already left the faith. The author does not raise the problem of people who wish to return to God after their apostasy. The words were to warn people who were considering apostasy. These people were reminded that God is a God of judgment and grace.

We also are tempted to fall away after hearing an old and worn message. Therefore, the church needs to hear not only the good news of Christ's sacrifice. There is a place for a word of judgment and a reminder that apostasy is the supreme insult to God's goodness.

Looking Forward (10:32-39)

If Hebrews is a model sermon, we notice that preaching contains both the good news of God's grace and the word of judgment that we dare not "trample" this grace. Hebrews 10:19-31 contains both the word of grace and the word of judgment. But before the author concludes his exhortation, there is one more feature to examine in 10:32-39.

"You have need of endurance," he tells his weary community (10:36). "Do not throw away your confidence" (10:35). "But we are not of those who shrink back and are destroyed" (10:39). Earlier the author appealed to this faltering community by reminding them of the enormity of God's gift (10:19-20) and the reality of his judgment (10:26-31). In 10:32-39 he makes one more appeal.

What can keep the church from throwing away its precious possession? In 10:32-39 the author reminds his audience of the promise of God that will make the pilgrimage worthwhile. "Do not throw away your confidence, *which has a great reward*" (10:35). "You have need of endurance, so that you may do the will of God *and receive what is promised*" (10:36).

The author even encourages his readers to endure by recalling what they have endured already. In the early days these Christians had "endured a hard struggle with sufferings" (10:32). Some had been imprisoned, abused, and robbed of their possessions (10:32-33). But they endured all of this because they knew that they had a different kind of possession, one which would abide forever (10:34). The one possesion which gave them power to endure was the one that no one could take from them.

It is no accident that a book addressed to weary Christians contains a significant number of references to God's reward or promise. The Christian is in the position of Moses, who also endured pain because he anticipated a reward (Heb. 11:26). Faith always involves a trust in God's reward (11:6). The Christian imitates others who have lived in faith because they believed in God's promise (6:20).

In our time of boredom with a story we have heard before, we need a "memory of better days." We should recall the hope which helped us overcome obstacles and endure either abuse or pain. We endured in the past because we knew that we were not struggling for a lost cause. Even when we are momentarily weary of our responsibilities and there are no immediate victories, hope helps us survive.

At first, this major section of Hebrews (8:1–10:39) may appear hard to understand to the modern reader. Its references to old customs may appear to say little to us as we struggle with the task of being a Christian. But if we notice the exhortation that comes at the end (10:19-39), we recognize that the author appeals to his readers to remain faithful by describing the greatness of what has been done for them by the sacrifice of Christ. The Christian is not only sustained by this great sacrifice. He lives also with the recognition of the tragedy of "trampling" this gift. He knows that this gift is only the beginning of God's promises. The Christian has a possession far too precious to throw away.

9

Keeping the Faith

"Faith is the assurance of things hoped for."

Hebrews 11

In the third century A.D., Celsus, the pagan philosopher, carried on a lively debate with Origen, the Christian scholar. The pagan philosopher tried to show that Christianity was untrue. He said that Christianity served only the superstitious and the simple-minded. If there was anything of substance to the Christian faith, Celsus argued, certainly it would have attracted a greater following. He was one of many educated people offended by Christian beliefs.

One characteristic which particularly offended ancient people was the Christian demand that people have faith in realities that no one could see or experience. The educated Greek required his students to examine all things using reason. Faith could too easily become a crutch for the simple minded who dared not face reality. Thus Christianity called for faith in its followers, but the pagans disdained this reliance on faith.

The old pagan argument seems modern. For many people, the church includes people who believe in a story and in a God who is far removed from the real world of their experience. Scientific advances have made God seem more and more remote from the world. Today's secularism concludes that the real world consists of our homes, our land, and those other material items that give us a sense of security. Indeed, we speak of papers that are locked away in a safety deposit box as our "securities."

This view affects the church. Our apathy toward the life of the church is probably the result of the unspoken belief that the *real world* is somewhere else. If it comes to a choice between our commitment to the church and the world we see, we easily demonstrate which of the two is the real world.

The sluggishness of the original readers of Hebrews was probably the result of a conviction that faith was impossible because they could not see or touch its reality. Frustration set in when the promises were not immediately fulfilled. Perhaps the fact that Christianity had turned out to be a long pilgrimage or a distance run had unsettled their convictions and left them with the feeling that faith had brought no security. Persecution and imprisonment (10:32-34) had left them at the point of "falling away" and "shrinking back" (10:39). Like Esau, they seemed ready to sell their birthright for a single meal from the *real world* (12:16-17). The only world apparent to them was the world they could see and touch. The realities of faith had become nothing more than a mirage.

The answer to their shrinking spirits, according to Hebrews 11, is faith. This great chapter might seem out of place in Hebrews, especially when we consider that the language of 5:1–10:39 concerned the tabernacle and the high priest. But chapter 11 is not out of place because the author has repeatedly told his discouraged readers that they need faith. They have been reminded that the people of God in the Old Testament started their pilgrimage well enough. They did not, however, inherit the promise because the message "was not mixed with faith" (4:2). The Israelites did not enter the land of promise because of their unbelief (3:19). Only those who believe enter God's rest (4:3). Finally, in 10:39, the author says, "We are not of those who shrink back and are destroyed, but of those who have faith and keep their souls."

What Does It Mean To Believe?

Faith may be one of the most misused words in our vocabulary. It is used to describe many different experiences. Some people say, "You have to believe," without telling us what is the object of faith. Perhaps they are simply saying that you must have faith in faith. On closer examination, faith turns out to be nothing more than positive thinking. For others, faith is a subjective feeling. The strength of one's faith can thus be easily tested by the extent of the emotional experience. Consequently, faith is absent if there is no overwhelming experience.

Other people reduce faith to the right opinions

on select issues. Thus faith is easily measured by one's response to a set of questions on certain problems.

The author of Hebrews is the only writer of the New Testament who defines faith. To a struggling community he wrote, "Now faith is the assurance of things hoped for, the conviction of things not seen" (11:1). This definition appears at the beginning of the chapter where he attempts to inspire his readers by reciting the names of faithful people of past generations.

The author uses two parallel expressions in Hebrews 11:1 to describe faith. It is "an assurance" (*hypostasis*) and a "conviction" (*elegchos*). The word for "assurance" in the Revised Standard Version is *hypostasis*. The King James Version appropriately uses "substance." The word literally means "that which stands beneath." It suggests a solid foundation or a place to stand and the security and stability of one who stands on solid ground.

As we review the author's advice to his readers, the idea of faith as having a place to stand becomes clearer. In 10:38-39, the writer contrasts faith with "shrinking back." In 6:11-12, faith is the equivalent of patience and reliability. Throughout the book there is concern for people who have lost their "place to stand." The author is worried that they will "drift away" (2:1) or "fall away" (3:12) from the faith. Faith is the opposite of "drifting away." The author says, "Faith is assurance." It is no subjective feeling.

The word for "conviction" (*elegchos*) is a legal term meaning "proof." It suggests the objective evidence and certainty needed in court. Faith, therefore is a "conviction" or a certainty. It is based on reality.

Things Hoped For, Things Not Seen

Most people build their lives on the realities of things that are visible. Television commercials present examples of the things in life that our culture takes to be real. "The good life" requires a new luxury car, new gadgets in the home, and new clothes. Our secular culture, with its extraordinary wealth, proclaims that reality is found in job promotions, new homes, and countless other status symbols that become the foundation of our lives. The "things that are seen" provide the place to stand in our culture. The shopping mall, with its multitude of objects for visual delight, testifies to those things that provide our security. Indeed, the premise behind a materialistic culture is that the "good life" can be built on the acquisition of the latest objects we do not need.

Against this background, the words of Hebrews 11:1 may shock us. Our "assurance" is found with "things hoped for" and "things not seen." For many people, nothing could be more uncertain than "things not seen." But for the author of Hebrews, the world we see is only a transient reality; it is not the real world at all. A materialistic culture places its trust in things that do not last. Only God's invisible world gives us a firm place to stand. This allows us to endure through adversity and accept disappointment. The Christian finds his security in the "abiding possession" (10:34), not in tangible objects.

This kind of faith makes demands. It separates us from the values of the culture in which we live.

At times it makes us appear ridiculous as we build our lives on values that are "not seen." In verses 3-40 the author surveys the great heroes of the past, extending from Abel to unnamed characters of a later period. They lived at different times and experienced quite different struggles. But they all shared something. The simple expression "by faith" describes their lives. These men and women, despite the difficulties of being God's people, found their own place to stand in the midst of adversity, and they did not find their security in tangible things.

Struggling people need heroes. In the time of crisis, Americans have called on names of their heroes. The example of Lincoln's lonely and agonizing decisions as president influenced almost inhuman effort from later generations. Churchill's defiance of all odds in his lonely struggle during World War II motivated others to live for a cause. The author of Hebrews knows the value of heroes for discouraged people. He said, "So that you may not be sluggish, but imitators of those who through faith inherit the promises (6:12)."

The tragedy of our time is that we have few heroes. Leading characters in films now are seldom heroes at all. They embrace no value higher than their own personal wishes. They have no cause worth the risk of their lives or the sacrifice of their pleasures. Perhaps our lack of heroes results from our belief that the real world consists of those things that are seen.

Where Are The Heroes

Henry Fairlie wrote an article in *Harper's* (Nov. 1978) called "Too Rich for Heroes." He suggested that

a society that has no heroes will soon grow en-
feebled. Its purposes will be less elevated; its as-
pirations less challenging; its endeavors less
strenuous. Its individual members will also be en-
feebled. They will 'hang loose' and 'lay back'
and, so mellowed out, the last thing of which
they wish to hear is heroism. They do not want to
be told of men and women whose example might
disturb them, calling them to effort and duty and
sacrifice or even the chance of glory. 'We have a
great many flutes and flageolets,' said Emerson,
'but not the sound of any fife' to summon us.

We need heroes to help us find values beyond ourselves. Alexander slept with the *Iliad* under his
pillow. He found his heroes in the noble spirits of
Achilles and Heracles. "If I have never been fascinated in childhood by my heroes and the won-
ders of life," Josiah Royce said in *The Philosophy
of Loyalty*, "it is harder to fascinate me later with
the call of duty."

Just as a civilization needs heroes to retain its
vitality and find values outside its own narrow in-
terests, the church also needs heroes. Consequently, the author of Hebrews presents his discouraged readers with a roll-call of ancient heroes
who had faced their discouragement. All of these
heroes exemplify, in one way or another, the definition of Hebrews 11:1. They founded their lives on
"things not seen." Noah, for example, built the ark
after he was warned about "things as yet not seen"
(11:8), and for this he became God's heir. Sarah
received the power to conceive "by faith" because
she trusted in God's promise (11:11). By faith the
patriarchs Isaac, Jacob, and Joseph invoked the
blessings of the future (11:20, 22). Moses gave up

the treasures of Egypt, choosing affliction instead because "he looked to the reward" (11:26). He left Egypt without fear "for he endured as seeing the invisible" (11:27). Faith, therefore, has always involved the "assurance of things not seen." As the author says, "He who comes to God must believe that He is and that He rewards those who seek him" (11:6). Many times we are told that faithful people lived in anticipation of a "homeland" (11:14) or a "city" (11:10). These men and women of faith trusted what others considered unreal.

"We need heroes to help us find values beyond ourselves."

When we take as our "assurance" what to others is unreal, we open ourselves to the struggle and insecurity of faith. Chapter 11 presents a consistent picture of the struggle of faith, for faith puts us into conflict with the values of every age. Noah, for example "condemned the world" (11:7) by his faith. The writer describes faithful people as pilgrims whose life on earth is "as in a foreign land" (11:9). Abraham "went out, not knowing where he was to go" (11:8). Similarly, Moses gave up on the enticements of the age for the sake of faith (11:25-26). Thus faith involves accepting the insecurity of being "a sojourner upon the earth" because we have found our "assurance" in "things not seen."

There are times, of course, when faith involves more than a life apart from one's own culture. The original readers learned that faith may involve suffering, imprisonment, and public abuse (10:32-33). The heroes of faith also left a legacy of daring and pain. Moses' parents were not afraid of the king's edict because they had faith (11:23). Likewise, Moses was not afraid of the edict of the king (11:27). Indeed, 11:32-38 presents a list of heroes who experienced suffering because of their faith. The author is able to recall heroic stories not only from the Old Testament, but from subsequent Jewish history. These people "died in faith" (11:13).

> Some were tortured, refusing to accept release, that they might rise again to a better life. Others suffered mocking and scourging, and even chains and imprisonment. They were stoned, they were sawn in two, they were killed with the sword.
> Hebrews 11:35-36

They knew that faith involved enduring, even when there was no immediate answer to their agony. They did not behave as people who believed that the real world is found among things we see or in accumulating new goods. Faith meant holding on in spite of all appearances.

Frustration And Faith

We can learn something about faith if we see the full dimensions of the emphasis on "things not seen." This is not a very popular part of Christianity because we would like to have assurances each day that faith "works." Some people seek these assurances in the form of economic benefits. Thus we are told that faith produces dividends in the form of new jobs, great bargains, and improved social life. For others, the constant assurances come in the form of peace of mind and in the absence of frustration and suffering. While it is true that there is "joy in believing," there is something very insidious about building our faith on tangible assurances. In Hebrews, faith can involve both frustration and suffering because it rests on "things not seen."

The author indicates the frustration of faith twice in chapter 11. In 11:13, he summarizes the experience of all of the heroes of faith. "These all died in faith, not having received what was promised, but having seen it and greeted it from afar . . ." In 11:39, after surveying history, the author says, "And these, though well-attested by their faith, did not receive what was promised." Faith as these examples suggest, does not receive instantaneous reassurance. The believer has to endure frustration and agony. He may wonder why God's promises do not seem fulfilled. Through all of this, faith involves "not having received what was promised" (11:13).

"What can the Christian do with frustration? Hebrews says we must learn to live with it."

Perhaps our lack of staying power is the result of our being unprepared for frustration. We may be unprepared for the problems of the local church. The tragedy that strikes us or our closest friends may appear to make a mockery of God's promises. If we believe that Christianity involves an endless succession of victories, frustration will result in our "shrinking back" from the demands of commitment. The promise of God may lead us to dream impossible dreams. But in reality, we may not "receive what is promised" in a whole lifetime on earth.

What can the Christian do with frustration? Hebrews says we must learn to live with it. The Christian does not give up at the first sign of despair. He must accept the frustration and keep the faith. George Buttrick said that our lives will experience all of the tension of a cello string which sings only when it is taut. This string is stretched between the infinite hope and the finite limitations of our lives. Life can produce its best music only when it lives with this kind of tension. We purchase "peace of mind," which is eagerly sought, only at the price of giving up on those promises which sustain us.

Jesus taught us to believe in the promises, but he also prepared us for frustration. He tells the parable of the sower, whose work consisted mainly in sowing seed which did not produce (Mark 4:3-9). He knew that his disciples would sometimes be like a helpless widow making her appeal before an unjust judge (Luke 18:1ff). Such stories indicate that Jesus anticipated the frustration of the Christian life.

As we follow the biblical record, we observe that the men of faith experienced deep frustration and despair. Job struggled with the questions of faith. Jeremiah lived in anguish over his calling. These people believed in "things not seen."

What does the church do with its frustration? We surrender to our own temporary values when we "shrink back." Faith involves holding on when our only source of security is found in "the things not seen." Certainly, the faith that began many centuries ago has survived, not because all of the faithful lived with constant victory, but because they held on in the presence of adversity. The church of today faces the same task. Our heroes from the past can teach us a valuable lesson.

10

Enduring Through Pain

"Let us run with perseverance."

Hebrews 12:1-17

Anyone who has ever watched athletes run a marathon will recognize this event as one of the most demanding contests ever devised. It is a test of endurance and speed. The brisk pace which Olympic runners maintain for the entire twenty-six miles amazes us. And the incredible endurance of the athletes also amazes us. To be able even to run the marathon is the result of painful hours spent acquiring the necessary stamina. But even experienced runners hit the "wall of pain" during the marathon. This moment may come around the twentieth mile, when the runner still has a long way to go. Undoubtedly his capacity to endure is most severely tested at this moment. The pain is discouraging. He may wonder if he can finish the course, and he begins to consider dropping out. If he finishes the course, it is because of his capacity to endure the "wall of pain" to the very end.

According to several witnesses in the New Testament, the Christian life is like an athletic contest. It may be compared to a fight 1(Cor. 9:26-27) or distance run (1 Cor. 9:26; 2 Tim. 4:7). The author of Hebrews uses the image of the athletic contest when he says, "Therefore, since we are surrounded by so great a cloud of witnesses, let us also lay aside every weight, and sin which clings so closely, and let us run with perseverance the race that is set before us" (Heb. 12:1). It was an appropriate illustration to use for this Christian community, whose life had already been compared to a pilgrimage (Heb. 3-4). Like the distance runner at the end of the course, they were fatigued. They had "drooping hands and weak knees" (12:12). They had reached their own wall of pain. They had begun the Christian pilgrimage long ago, but now they were discovering that the Christian life was a distance run and not a sprint.

"You have need of endurance," they were told (10:36). To have faith means to hold on in the midst of pain, doubting moods, and promises that have not been realized (11:13). Some of the readers were dropping out of the race and neglecting and despising their great hope because they, like the distance runner, were discouraged by the presence of pain.

The illustration of the distance run may not be popular today because our culture seems to expect a life without pain. It is popular to expect pills for our stress, a drink in the evening to settle the nerves, and drugs to dull the senses. It is little wonder, then, that the Christianity often advertised is expected to be painless. We often hear of a Christianity that acts as a magic wand to take away our pain. It is supposed to open new doors that make us rich and popular. Or it is like magic that lifts us up out of a situation of stress and promises relief from pain.

But the Christian life does involve pain and discouragement and makes us wonder if we can finish the course. The first sign of pain could be devastating, especially if we have been led to believe that our Christianity will bring only relief from stress.

Paul experienced pain in his Christian life. The thorn in his flesh (2 Cor. 12:7ff.) was a chronic ailment with no relief. We also experience pain because of our faith. The readers of Hebrews experienced it. Just after their baptism they "endured a hard struggle with sufferings." They had been held up to public abuse and scorn, and their property had been plundered (10:32-34). Many of the readers had begun to ask, "How long can we go on?" The struggle was discouraging.

How do you endure when you hit the "wall of pain" in your Christian life? The author of Hebrews never suggested that Christianity would relieve pain. Instead, he reminded a tired community that we are all involved in a great athletic contest we must endure to the end. The word for "struggle" (*athlēsis*) in 10:32 is the term for an athletic contest. Then in 12:1 he says, "Let us run with perseverance the race that is set before us."

The Heritage Of Pain

How shall we continue in a race when we are tired? The author of Hebrews pictures for his readers a great stadium where we are "surrounded by a great cloud of witnesses" (12:1). It is as if the church is on the field. The dense mass of people looks like a cloud above them in the stadium. The witnesses are not merely neutral observers. They have come to cheer us on. We are strengthened in the moment of pain by the encouragement of the partisan crowd.

And we should be encouraged by this partisan crowd. These witnesses are our predecessors. Before the author encourages his readers to run the race, he describes the heroes of the past who were "well attested" by their faith (11:39). The word for "witnesses" (*martus*) appeared in chapter 11 (verses 2, 4, 5, and 39) to describe people whom God has approved (or "attested"). The men and women of the Old Testament knew their share of frustration (11:13), risk, and pain in believing. As the author concludes,

> For time would fail me to tell of Gideon, Barak, Samson, Jephthah, of David and Samuel and the prophets—who through faith conquered kingdoms, enforced justice, received promises, stopped the mouths of lions, quenched raging fire, escaped the edge of the sword, won strength out of weakness, became mighty in war, put foreign armies to flight . . . Some were tortured . . . others suffered scourging, and even chains and imprisonment. They were stoned, they were sawn in two . . . destitute, afflicted, ill-treated— of whom the world was not worthy.

We have, therefore, a heritage of pain. To be faithful is to hold on despite pain. Others ran the race before us like noble, disciplined athletes. They too considered giving up, but they completed their course. And now they depend on us to finish the course, for without us their work would be incomplete. "Apart from us they should not be perfect" (11:40). So the "great cloud of witnesses" urges us to be faithful in the midst of pain.

However, the greatest example of faithfulness in

the midst of pain is Jesus, the "pioneer and perfecter of faith." The "pioneer" (*archēgos*, 2:10 and 12:2) was the "trailblazer" or founder who opened the way. Jesus first traveled the way we now travel and demonstrated that it was possible. He has run the race before us and faced our pain, frustration, and disappointments. He "endured the cross" when the struggle seemed to be futile. Indeed, the Christian faith had its beginning in the struggle to endure pain. Jesus is the pioneer to whom we look for a model for endurance. Consequently, the author says, "Looking to Jesus . . . ."

The athlete distracted away from his goal is destined to become discouraged and drop out. His only hope of maintaining his determination is to keep his eyes intently on the goal. Likewise, discouraged Christians are told to look to Jesus. He has traveled the road ahead of us, and He has reached the destination.

George Buttrick reminded us that Christ never sought escape from pain.

> One wonders if our all-too-easy cult of "personality" and success, though it is preached in some churches, ever remembers that the Jesus (whom it is supposed to preach) was nailed up by the hands and died as a common criminal . . . He walked with open eyes straight into pain, and refused any opiate . . . He told us that the secret of pain is not on this side of pain, least of all for the man who tries to sidestep it, but clean through pain—on the other side.[1]

Thus neither Jesus, Paul, nor the author of Hebrews offered an opiate for pain. There was no promise of a quick solution or easy victory. Faith was not the immediate release from physical or emotional agony. Indeed, faith could even mean the beginning of pain. It can involve living with physical ailments, as Paul did, or bearing abuse from others, as Jesus did.

There is a scene in George Bernard Shaw's play *St. Joan* where the bishop tells Joan that he fears that she is in love with religion. "Is there any harm in it?" Joan asked. "No," said the bishop, "but it could be dangerous." He remembered that Christianity began with a cross.

"We can face the wall of pain because there is a goal ahead."

When the athlete hits the wall of pain, there is nothing he can do but endure it if he intends to finish. People in our culture do not want to be told to *endure* anything unpleasant. But the story of the cross is the one great story of endurance. Jesus "endured the cross" (12:2), and he "endured hostility from sinners" (12:3). The cross reminds us that pain is not taken away instantly. The word "perseverance" (*hupomonē*) is the same term which is used for the endurance of Jesus.

Job and Paul displayed different attitudes about suffering. In the Old Testament, Job never renounces God, but he at least questions His fairness. There are moments when he begs for an umpire between himself and God (Job 9:33), and he doubts that God cares. But Paul could approach suffering with far greater equanimity, even daring to rejoice in his sufferings (Rom. 5:2, Col. 1:24). But why the difference between Paul and Job? Could it be that Paul had the advantage of having seen in Jesus Christ that suffering has meaning? He realized that God shared in our suffering

109

through Jesus. We must also "look to Jesus" to recognize that we do not suffer alone.

It would be futile to suggest that pain must be endured if there is no good news at the end. Viktor Frankl, a physician who spent years in a Nazi concentration camp, said, "We can bear almost any 'how' if only we have a 'why.'" We need to know that something lies beyond our suffering. Frankl describes his own battle for survival in *Man's Search for Meaning*. The hope that the concentration camp was not the end gave him the will to survive. The glimmer of hope that he might outlive the terror and continue his research helped him survive.

There is also hope for the Christian. The Christ who "endured the cross" now is "seated at the right hand of God." We can face the wall of pain because there is a goal ahead.

The Education God Provides

Alexander Solzhenitsyn's commencement address at Harvard in 1978 described the vast difference in the affluent people of the Western world and the people of Eastern Europe. "It has become possible (in the West) to raise young people according to these ideals (of material well-being), leading them to physical splendor, happiness, possession of material goods, money, and leisure, to an almost unlimited freedom of enjoyment." Yet, he says, there is a danger in such constant freedom. "Even biology knows that habitual extreme safety and well-being are not advantageous for a living organism." Human beings who experience no pain become weaker.

On the other hand, Solzhenitsyn said, imagine the deprivation of those who do not live in a free country and who expect no right to a life free from struggle:

> Six decades for our people and three decades for the people of Eastern Europe: during that time we have been through a spiritual training far in advance of Western experience. Life's complexity and mortal weight have produced stronger, deeper and more interesting characters than those generated by standardized Western well-being.

The onslaught of pain which makes us wonder about our existence may, in fact, be the very thing which develops our character. The author of Hebrews makes this observation. Just as his readers, like tired runners, started to wonder about their future, he answers with an "exhortation" from Proverbs (Heb. 12:5-6, Prov. 3:11):

> My son, do not regard lightly the discipline of the Lord,
> nor lose courage when you are punished by him.
> For the Lord disciplines him whom He loves,
> and chastises every son whom He receives.

We cannot tolerate suffering without purpose. But we can accept suffering if we are assured that God is our Father, and that He is working out His purposes. Alan Paton wrote in *Creative Suffering* that it is almost as if we said to God, "Some say you are cruel, and we confess that the cruelty of the world troubles us, so that we have moments of doubt; but of your goodness we have no doubt, having seen it in the life of Jesus; therefore we put our lives in your hands, so that you may use them for the sake of others."[2] The Christian who has come to the wall of pain need not give up on God. He knows that God is dealing with us as sons (Heb. 12:5). Even Jesus, the unique Son, "learned obedience through suffering" (Heb. 5:8). So it is natural that we, his brothers (Heb. 2:12), also learn through suffering.

Ancient people knew neglected and illegitimate children never received a sound education. But fathers who genuinely loved their children exercised discipline on them. Education that did not include corporal punishment was unheard of in ancient times (Prov. 13:24, 22:15, 23:12-14). The one word *paideia* in Greek means education, discipline, and chastisement because education included correction. Consequently, the author of Hebrews tells his discouraged readers, "It is for discipline that you have to endure" (Heb. 12:7). Suffering does not mean that God has ceased to care for us; it may be the training provided by a caring Father.

"Suffering does not mean that God has ceased to care for us; it may be the training provided by a caring Father."

Many things along the Christian pilgrimage cause us pain. In addition to physical pain which tests us, there may be psychic pain from maintaining our Christian commitment in a world which disdains our values. There is the pain of the many crises which face the church and the struggle to be patient when these crises make life unpleasant. Undoubtedly, the easiest thing for us may be to drop out and avoid the pain. Certainly we are not prepared for it if we expect Christianity to offer only perpetual "victorious living." But the history of salvation shows that Christianity was born with a Savior who endured the cross, and that it has continued because of the perseverance of those who chose to endure God's discipline (Heb. 12:7).

God chooses not to remove pain from his believers. If He did, we might serve Him for the wrong reasons. But neither has he left us to fear that our suffering is useless. He has demonstrated in Jesus Christ that we are his sons, and that our elder brother has already "endured the cross" and moved through the barrier of pain to the right hand of God. We too know that we can finish the course because Jesus endured discipline without giving up.

---

[1]George Buttrick, *God, Pain and Evil* (Abingdon, 1966), p. 150.
[2]Alan Paton, *Creative Suffering* (Pilgrim Press), p. 17.

11

Going
to Church

"*You have come to Mount Zion and to the city of
the living God.*"

Hebrews 12:18-29

In an amusing scene in Mark Twain's *Tom
Sawyer*, Tom had gone to Sunday school and
church at the demand of Aunt Polly. After Sunday
school Tom and his brother Sid go to the audito-
rium to sit under the watchful eye of Aunt Polly.
Next we read a boy's description of public worship. Announcements are made from a "list would
stretch out to the crack of doom." The prayer is
"generous in its details." Tom is so familiar with
the prayer that he knows it by heart, and so he
recognizes and resents any new additions to it. The
preacher's sermon "drones on monotonously
through an argument that is so prosy that many a
head began to nod." The service bores Tom.

Perhaps Tom's descriptions remind us of similar

experiences in our own lives, especially during childhood. We too have experienced public worship when it was less than invigorating. We remember times when worship seemed to be designed to dull the senses. Many people expect worship to be dull, trivial, and boring. They use the time to plan next week's activities or compose the invitation list to the next social event. As a performance, worship hardly ranks with a good drama. For excitement, it does not seem to compare with a football game. In its passionate devotion to a cause, it may not compare favorably with a political convention.

So why go to church? That question might not have been asked in many communities a generation ago because it was commonly assumed that church attendance was important. But now many people ask the question. Some have always attended church by habit. Others have attended because it was expected within the community or social circle. Some have never been a part of church life and they wonder about the value of church attendance. For many people, attendance at worship seems to have little relationship to God's demands for the Christian life. Thus, "going to church" appears to be a custom of people who insist on maintaining an old tradition.

Only Hebrews, among all the books of the New Testament, provides an answer to this question. The other books of the New Testament probably do not deal with this problem because the importance of church attendance was never questioned. Early Christians knew they must be present in the frequent—even daily—gatherings of the disciples (Acts 2:46, 1 Cor. 14:26).

The Christians who first read Hebrews had developed a disturbing custom of neglecting the assembly (Heb. 10:25). We do not know all of the reasons why they were not attending church. But Hebrews tells us that their neglect of the assembly was a part of a deep spiritual weariness that afflicted the community. They had become "sluggish in hearing" (5:11), and they were in danger of committing apostasy (3:12, 6:4-5). They had "drooping hands and weak knees" (12:12). One of the signs of their boredom and weariness was that they no longer attended church. The author said to this early church, "Not forsaking the assembly, as the manner of some is, but encouraging each other all the more as you see the day approaching" (Heb. 10:25).

Is Anything Happening?

Why had these people stopped coming to worship? They were bored and tired. Their reasons for neglecting the assembly must have been very much like our own. Perhaps they found the worship too simple and plain—hardly a match for the elaborate pagan rituals down the street! The worship might have appeared distressingly unspectacular. To them church consisted merely of singing hymns and preaching the word (Heb. 13:15). And so they might have complained that "nothing happened there." There was little pageantry or excitement so these Christians expressed their boredom by dropping out of church. They were tired of the routine.

It is a tragedy when we see our acquaintances drop out. Dropping out of public worship is not like withdrawing from a club. It is more like throwing away a precious treasure. It is like choosing a worthless trinket we could have now in place of something of far greater value. Thus the readers are told, "Therefore lift your drooping hands and strengthen your weak knees" (12:12). We are like people on a pilgrimage to the promised land. It would be a tragedy to drop out considering the goal that lies just ahead. And it would be a tragedy to permit our friends to drop out because we are a community. We make the road easier for those who are lame (Heb. 12:13). We "see to it that no one fails to obtain the grace of God" (Heb. 12:15) because we are our brother's keeper. Esau threw away his precious inheritance for a single meal (Heb. 12:16), but we should try to see that no one makes the same mistake by dropping out of church.

We might expect the author to encourage his readers to return to church by suggesting that worship be made more exciting. Or we might expect him to encourage the church to match the worship to the tastes of the audience. Instead, he has another "why" to church attendance. In Hebrews 12:18-29 he describes what happens every time we come to worship—even when we are not visibly moved aesthetically or emotionally. These beautiful words might have been read to a small congregation meeting in someone's home. Nothing about that assembly would look very impressive. Yet the little congregation hears that something very important is happening.

What happens when we worship together?

> You have not come to what may be touched, a blazing fire, and darkness, and gloom, and a tempest, and the sound of a trumpet . . . But you have come to Mount Zion, to the city of the living God, the heavenly Jerusalem, and to innumerable angels in festal array, and to the assembly of the

first born who are enrolled in heaven, and to a God who is judge of all, and to the spirits of the just men made perfect, and to Jesus, the mediator of a new covenant . . . ."

Hebrews 12:18, 22-23

Meeting God

The Israelites came before God in awe and trembling at Mount Sinai. They stood at a mountain that they dared not even touch. But Christians, who meet in small congregations that may seem plain and unimpressive, have come to Mount Zion. The word "You have come" (*proserchomai*) was the Old Testament word for the high priest who approached God at the temple to sacrifice, for only he had access to God. But now in Jesus Christ we all have access to God through the blood of Jesus (Heb. 4:16, 10:19-22). It is one of the great blessings of the Christian faith to be invited to "draw near" to God in worship.

Have you ever thought what happens in worship when you are not in the mood and when the singing and preaching are not pleasing? It may not look like much, but when we worship we come before God. The author may have said, "Do you know with whom you are meeting?"

It is always tempting for us to judge the quality of worship by the beauty of the setting or the impressiveness of what we see and hear. The Israelites at Mount Sinai had approached God in a scene that was tangible and terrifying to the sense . But our worship is different. "You have not come to what may be touched." Our worship may not look impressive, but we still are in God's presence.

We are not told, "You might come to Mount Zion." It is not a case of some day meeting in the presence of God and the angels. Rather, this is what happens every time we meet for worship. If only we could appreciate our heritage!

The late T. W. Manson once wrote,

> Many people assume that if they are not consciously uplifted by going to church there is no reason why they should continue to go. The Jewish way of looking at it was much more concerned with whether or not these acts of worship were acceptable to God ... The question whether he wanted to go to the synagogue at a set time had nothing to do with the case. His business was to be there ... It is quite easy, as we all know, for dutiful worship to degenerate into the mechanical performance of rites that have ceased to mean anything to the performer. I do not think that is a serious danger today. We are more exposed to the danger, from which the Jew was set free, of ceasing to worship because we are never in the mood, or because our half-hearted attempts produce no immediate or exciting emotional results.[1]

We need to hear, "You have come . . . ." Something happens in worship that does not depend on us—the presence of God.

Worship As The Great Encounter

The author's list of encounters which take place in worship may overwhelm us. "You have come to Mount Zion, the city of the living God, the heavenly Jerusalem, to myriads of angels in festal array, to the church of the first born written in the heavens . . . ." These little communities might have had difficulty believing this. It did not look

119

impressive. But they were in touch with spiritual reality.

Worship may take place away from the regular meeting place. Indeed, a life dedicated to God can be called a "spiritual worship" (Rom. 12:1). But we need special times for worship. William Temple said, "All life ought to be worship." And he added, "We know quite well there is no chance it will be worship unless we have times when we have worship and nothing else."

"If we do not have special times of worship, we lose our perspective on life and our sense of values."

If we do not have special times of worship, we lose our perspective on life and our sense of values. We begin to think that the only things that are real are the things we can see and touch. We should be disturbed by living in a society which has lost its sense of God and of knowing anything beyond its material existence. Tagore, the great Indian mystic, wrote a poem comparing our lives to a narrow lane lined with high buildings with only a single strip of blue sky above. The lane, which sees the blue sky for only a few minutes a day, asks herself—is it real? But the dust and rubbish never rouse her to question. The noise of traffic, the jolting carts, the refuse, the smoke—these she accepts as the real and actual things of life. Soon she ceases to wonder about the strip of blue above. This, Tagore says, is what our life is like. We only accept the things that we see as real. We forget the streak of blue above. In worship—in the singing of

120

hymns and in the preaching of the word—we have come to the heavenly Jerusalem.[2]

We think of worship as an encounter with our friends in the local community, but it is more than that. "You have come to myriads of angels in festal array and to the assembly of the first born enrolled in heaven, . . . to the spirits of the just men made perfect." We are uniting in a heritage and sharing in a fellowship with those who have lived before us ("the spirits of the just men made perfect"). The heroes of faith (ch. 11) are the "great cloud of witnesses" (12:1) who sit in the stadium and cheer us on as we finish our race. We are in danger of living for the moment and losing our contact with the past. But in worship we meet with those who have preceded us.

". . . In worship we meet with those who have preceded us."

But worship is not just an encounter with our predecessors. It is a world-wide fellowship: "the church of the firstborn who are enrolled in heaven." Communities like our own meet around the world to sing, "Christ the Lord is risen." In countless languages they recall the death of Jesus by sharing in the Lord's Supper. It is good to be loyal to our own congregation. But it is also good to know that in worship we meet with Christians around the world.

Worship is also an encounter with God. "You have come to a judge who is God of all, . . . to Jesus, the mediator of a new covenant." Even when worship is routine, he is present. In ancient

121

Israel, he was present despite fire, darkness, and gloom (Heb. 12:18). But for us He is present in the study of the word and in the offering of praise. Our God is "a consuming fire" (Heb. 12:29), and we come before him in awe.

"When we neglect worship, we throw away the lasting possession."

We do not meet only God. We meet the "sprinkled blood that speaks more graciously than the blood of Abel." A society that has lost its sense of worship has been left all alone without a word of comfort or direction from outside and without anyone to offer a word of forgiveness. In worship the blood of Christ "speaks" to us. We come as sinners, having failed to live up to our standard. We come having failed as parents, sons, daughters, husbands, and wives. We come with spiritual pride which makes us feel secure and separates us from others. In worship we discover the One who speaks to us words of consolation and forgiveness.

Realizing that worship is an assembly with God and the angels—and that we are already enjoying the presence of God, it seems incredible that anyone would be careless or flippant about going to church. To neglect worship to enjoy the things we can see and touch is absurd. But like Esau, we are tempted to throw away the lasting gift for the one we can have now (Heb. 12:16). Or, like the children of Israel, we give up on God's promise for the sake of ease and comfort now. When we neglect worship, we throw away the lasting possession. Thus the readers are told, "Do not refuse him who is speaking."

Living In A Changing World

Alvin Toffler's book *Future Shock* describes the unsettling effects of living in a world where nothing is stable. Rapid changes in technology mean we may have to learn new job skills several times in a lifetime. The mobility of our society involves us and our neighbors in so many moves that we are never able to have acquaintances for a long period of time.

Beliefs and moral standards seem to be in constant confusion. Today's truth is outdated tomorrow. Today's standard is only a temporary thing. Toffler says that such changes can be destructive to us unless we find "stability zones" to give security to their lives. There are many changes around us which we cannot prevent. But we need one area of our life that is stable to give us a sense of security.

The author of Hebrews tells his tired community that Christians have the anchor for our lives. He pictures, at the end of chapter 12, the end of everything. He talks about the world's destruction and the end of all material things in 12:27. But he also refers to the abiding of those heavenly realities which "cannot be shaken." And then he says to the community, "Therefore let us be grateful for receiving a kingdom that cannot be shaken, and thus let us offer to God acceptable worship, with reverence and awe; for our God is a consuming fire" (12:28f). In a world filled with change, we find in worship a "kingdom that cannot be shaken."

---

[1] *Ethics and the Gospel*
[2] James Stewart, *The Wind of the Spirit*, (New York: Abingdon, 1968) p. 126.

12

Living Outside the Camp

"Let us go forth to him outside the camp."

Hebrews 13

"The world for Christ in our generation." It is an old dream, a dream held by more than one generation. Many of us recall the optimism which prevailed when some kind of breakthrough was near. There are still places where Christians maintain exciting ministries to reach out with the message of Christ. But there are also alarming signs which raise questions about our ability to survive as a community of faith. Congregations should be disturbed at the attrition rate of young people. We should also be concerned with the long range effects of the diminishing influence of religion in our society on the survival of the church.

The seriousness of these problems became especially apparent to me when I was a minister for a small church in the nation's largest city. Most of the adult members were transplanted from smaller cities of the South which were far less secularized than their new home. They were never really "at home" in the city, but the church was one place where they felt comfortable. Their children, however, had quite a different experience. They had few memories of life anywhere else. They had grown up in this very secular environment. And by the time they became teenagers, they recognized that their religious life made them very different from their peers. They held beliefs that were largely unintelligible to their friends, and they were expected to maintain a lifestyle and a set of moral standards that were radically different from others. This sense of being different—of belonging to this "strange sect"—threatened their Christian identity.

I do not recall seeing anyone give up the faith because intellectual problems became too unbearable. They did not drop out because they had examined the evidence for Christianity and found it unbelievable. But I did see several young Christians struggling to hold a set of beliefs which "no one believes anymore." Unfortunately, in too many instances it was a losing struggle.

"Survival was never very difficult when religion was socially acceptable."

I mention this not because it demonstrates the hopeless spiritual condition of a great American city. I mention it because it describes a condition in which we may all find ourselves. Many of us recall when it was easier to keep the faith because religion was more popular than it is today. The people in our neighborhood went to church on Sunday morning as we did. Christian moral standards were understood and appreciated. References to the importance of religious faith were often made in school and by government officials. This popularity of religious commitment served as a prop to help us survive. Survival was never very difficult where religion was socially acceptable.

An Assault On Christian Values

But most of these props have been removed, and secularization characterizes major American cities. The media consistently undermine Christian values. We wonder whether the wave of bizarre sexual relationships portrayed in the movies is creating a new set of values or simply reflecting the prevailing standards of our society. At any rate, it portrays a style of life that is an assault on Christian values. We may begin to believe that the lifestyle on the screen is normal behavior. When we see a standard of sexual behavior where fidelity is considered a thing of the past, we may begin to question our own beliefs. The effect of constant exposure to these assaults on Christian values leaves us vulnerable and wondering if we are out of step with the rest of the world. This trend poses a serious problem for the church. Many people find it very difficult to keep the faith when "no one believes those things anymore."

Sociologists report that much of what we believe and know comes from society around us, not from our own investigation and analysis. From earliest childhood we come to believe certain things about the world because "everyone knows it is that way." We believe them because it seems silly to question what everyone knows is true. If you hold to a point of view that is largely unacceptable to the larger group, you begin to question any view that is contrary to "what everyone knows."

Sociologist Peter Berger gives a vivid illustration of the effects on us when we hold a minority position. Imagine a person coming to America from a culture in which "everyone knows" that the stars influence human events. When he arrives and begins to espouse such a view, he will be treated with amusement and surprise. Before long he will wonder if something is wrong with him. After a while he may decide that life would be easier if he simply kept his views to himself. Finally, he would probably have doubts about his views that would lead him to give up on them.

The situation could also be reversed. An American who is stranded in a land where "everyone knows" that the stars influence human behavior might also find his position tottering. Even though what he believes is true, he finds it threatening to believe what is considered absurd by others because we need a community to support and sustain our beliefs.

One of the gravest threats to the survival of the church, I believe, is not that some new piece of scientific evidence will shatter our convictions. It is the experience of holding to a set of views that are unacceptable to the majority of the people. Like the psalmist, we may be asking, "How do you sing the Lord's song in a foreign land?" Do we have a strategy for survival?

We can learn from another minority group which faced these same problems centuries ago. The early church never enjoyed the props of respectability and social acceptability. The proclamation of a crucified Savior was "folly" to the majority of the people of that time. Early Christianity took its shape at a time when the Christians were not to be "conformed to this world" (Rom. 12:1). The readers of Hebrews never knew the props of respectability and acceptability. Their situation was more extreme than our own. They faced persecution and suffering (10:32). Apparently this situation of being "outside" public acceptability led some of the members to give up the faith because some had ceased to attend the worship. The author told the entire church that they needed endurance, and he gave them a strategy for survival.

Jesus Died Outside The Camp

In Hebrews 13:12 the author reminds his people that Christianity did not begin with the protective arm of public acceptance. Jesus never received any medals as "outstanding young man of the year" in Jerusalem. There was no "eternal flame" for Jesus at the Jerusalem National Cemetery. There was no state funeral, nor any kind words from a chief of state. The author reminds his readers that Jesus died "outside the camp" at Jerusalem.

Jesus died at a place "not far from the city" (John 19:20) where criminals were executed. No experience could have been further from public acceptance. The author states, "Jesus endured shame" (Heb. 12:2) in his crucifixion. People trained in the Jewish tradition recall that the remains of the animals which had been sacrificed were "burned outside the camp" (Lev. 16:27), and that those who burned them also became unclean. "Everyone knew" that Jesus had died a shameful death.

Early Christians were probably uneasy about declaring that their Savior had died on a cross because it was the ancient equivalent of the electric chair. "Everyone knew" that good men did not die on crosses. Paul said, "Jews demand signs and Greeks seek wisdom" (1 Cor. 1:22). The story of a crucified Savior was a "stumbling block to Jews and folly to Gentiles" (1 Cor. 1:23). Ancient people did not always like to be reminded that Christianity began without the props of public acceptance, but the author of Hebrews will not let us forget.

George McDonald wrote in *Only One Way Left*,

I am recovering the claim that Jesus was not crucified in a cathedral between two candles, but on a cross between two thieves, on the town garbage heap . . . at the kind of place where cynics talk smut, and thieves curse, and soldiers gamble. Because that is where he died and that is what he died about. And that is where churchmen should be and what churchmanship is about.

We think we need public respectability to maintain our faith. But when ancient people were disturbed by their minority status, they were reminded that Jesus died "outside the camp" of public acceptance. He died alone, rejected by his own people. His cross has always been a "scandal" (1 Cor. 1:23) to those who demand that our religious faith be "respectable" in the eyes of the prevailing culture.

The church needs to be reminded often that Jesus died "outside the camp" of his own people, and that faith involved "enduring shame" (Heb. 12:2). Jesus, the one who endured despite the shame of the cross, is the "pioneer" who led the way (Heb. 2:9). He is a reminder to his people that they too can endure the loneliness of believing. Hebrews 11 says there is a whole "cloud of witnesses" (12:1) who have "gone out" (11:8) and experienced the loneliness of faith. Our survival depends on our recognizing that the previous heroes

of faith did not have the props of public respectability. It was always a faith that involved being
"outside."

"Let Us Go Forth To Him, Hearing Abuse For Him"

If Jesus died "outside the camp" of respectability, it would be absurd to imagine that the Christian
would be spared the experience of sharing his fate.
The life of faith has always involved "bearing
abuse" (Heb. 11:26) for the sake of Christ. Jesus
talked about the necessity of "bearing his cross"
(Mark 8:34). The readers of Hebrews had already
suffered on account of the faith (10:32-34). Their
faith had already taken them "outside" community
values in a world where Christianity seemed absurd to most people. The striking thing about the
advice in Hebrews 13:13 is the reminder that our
legitimate place is outside the camp. Christ is our
pioneer who calls us to follow him to the cross.
When our lifestyle weds us too closely to prevailing standards, we have not accompanied our pioneer "outside the camp."

This advice may seem inappropriate for us because we are not being imprisoned for our faith.
But there is a vital message for the church today in
the author's advice. In a time when our having to
be "outside" the values of the day threatens the
survival of the church, the author reminds us that
Christians have always followed their Lord "outside the camp." The demands that are placed on us
are no different from the demands that have been
placed on Christians in every generation.

What does it mean to be "outside the camp" in
today's world? Someone has said that a Christian is
able to "swim against the stream." The Christian

has found his or her identity in Jesus Christ so that he or she is not threatened by being different. In today's world, living "outside the camp" may involve the willingness to live in a society that "looks out for number one." Or it may mean the willingness to rely on God in a culture which ignores Him. It may mean holding on to our sexual morality in a world which disregards these values. Our strategy for survival must include an acknowledgement that Christ calls us to take on a set of standards that appears to be foolish. Paul said, "Don't let the world squeeze you into its mold" (Rom. 12:2, J.B. Phillips).

There is no other strategy but to follow Jesus "outside the camp." If we were to decide that the appropriate thing to do is reflect the values of our society, we would discover that the church would be offering nothing which could not be found elsewhere. A church that chose always to be "inside the camp" of public acceptance would not survive. It would have no word to offer.

Sociologists say it is very difficult to maintain our beliefs for long unless our values are reinforced by a group of people who hold the same convictions. It is difficult to keep our identity if we must be alone. The author of Hebrews says, "Therefore let us go forth to him outside the camp, bearing abuse for him." We are not asked to be alone! We have a community that nurtures and supports our Christian values. When we worship and study together, we encourage each other (3:13, 10:25) and provide the help that allows us to survive. It may be difficult to maintain our beliefs if we must maintain them alone. But we do not have to survive alone because we go "outside the camp" together.

131

"We Seek The City Which Is To Come"

If all of our efforts to keep the faith were certain to come to nothing, we certainly would never survive. Nothing is more futile than a lost cause. Viktor Frankl observed from his experiences in the Nazi prison camp, "We can withstand almost any 'how' if only we have a 'why.' " If there is a goal at the end of our struggles, we can endure almost anything. But if we are sacrificing for a lost cause, we will not endure long.

The author of Hebrews reminds his readers, "For here we have no lasting city, but we seek the city which is to come" (13:14). We are not enduring for a lost cause because the way of struggle is also the way of victory. Jesus endured the shame of the cross, but now our pioneer is seated at the right hand of God (Heb. 12:2). He died outside the camp, but his death was the way to victory. It was never a lost cause!

"Christians share the loneliness of Jesus because his cause is not lost."

The world's values might lead us to believe that the really permanent and lasting things of life are within our culture and the standards of the day. But we can go outside the camp of this culture because we know that the really "abiding city" is not here at all. The lost cause is the standard of our society that looks inviting. Thus Christians share the loneliness of Jesus because his cause is not lost.

We do have a strategy for survival. It does not include accepting the lifestyle and values that are constantly placed before our eyes. We will be able to survive by being "outside the camp." And by going "outside the camp" together we can support each other along the way.

13

Renewing Our Commitment

> *"For we share in Christ, if only we hold our first confidence firm to the end."*

Hebrews 3:14

"When the Son of Man comes, will he find faith on the earth?" This is the concluding sentence in one of the parables of Jesus (Luke 18:1-8). He pictured the church as a defenseless widow who called for vindication to a heartless judge. Her one weapon, in the presence of frustration, was her persistence, and it finally brought her vindication. Perhaps Jesus was suggesting that God at times seems silent and foreign to us—even as heartless as an unprincipled judge. But God is faithful to his people who believe. The essential question of the parable confronts believers in every age: will they persist in believing in times of frustration and hopelessness? The question certainly is appropriate for today's church.

For the author of Hebrews, the answer to the

question was not obvious. His exhortations remind the readers that their survival is not assured. He punctuates his message with "if" clauses (3:6, 14) which remind them of their obligations to keep the faith. The same counsel could easily have been directed at contemporary Christians. When the author says, "You have need of endurance" (10:36), his words remind us that our struggles are not new. Perhaps what is most unusual about Hebrews is its author's prescription for their "drooping hands and weak knees" (12:12). His word to a tired church suggests an approach to the problem of apathy which would probably be untried in most congregations. We can discover insights for our own situation from a letter to a tired church. These insights from Hebrews need to be heard by weary congregations today.

What God Has Done

We observe in Hebrews that a letter intended to awaken a weary congregation is composed of more than just exhortations summoning his readers to a greater effort. The book, of course, abounds in imperatives. But more attention is given to reminding Christians of what they "have" in Jesus Christ. It is no accident that the book often speaks in the indicative, and that a frequent word in Hebrews is the verb "have." Readers are motivated first by reminders of their salvation in Jesus Christ (for references to the word "have" or "having," see 4:14-15, 8:1, 10:19, 13:14).

Hebrews contains a fascinating array of images that suggest that Christians can easily lose their grasp on a way of life that brings security. When the author warns his readers against "drifting away" (2:1), his illustration suggests someone at sea who is left to drift along without anything for security. A similar image is suggested by the warning against being "led away" (13:9, literally "carried away"). The author suggests that what the readers need most is a place of security if they are to keep the faith.

We too can find ourselves aimlessly "drifting away" in a time when we have seen many changes in beliefs and moral standards. The rate at which everything changes can be very threatening if we do not have a secure place to stand. With this in mind, the book of Hebrews develops a theme that should be helpful. In Jesus Christ we find what is firm and unshakable. The Greek word for "firm" (*bebaios*) is used frequently in Hebrews (2:2; 3:14; 6:16; 9:17). The word is also used to describe our Christian hope as "an anchor of the soul" (6:19) that is sure and steadfast.

Closely related to those words suggesting that our faith is "firm" are the many expressions in Hebrews that affirm that what we have in Jesus Christ is "abiding" and stable. On two occasions, for instance, Jesus Christ is described as the one who is "the same" (1:12, 13:8). On other occasions, the author describes Him as the one who abides forever (7:3, 24). He also describes our Christian hope in words that suggest stability. Our hope involves an "abiding possession" (10:34). Or, in the words of 13:14, we anticipate an "abiding city." According to 12:27-28, the church receives from God "an unshakable kingdom." Those who have an anchor for their lives need not "drift away" because they have found something that continues forever.

John writes about a scene in the ministry of

Jesus where "many of the disciples drew back and no longer went about with him" (John 6:66). When Jesus asked if the remaining disciples would also go away, Peter answered, "Lord, to whom shall we go? You have the words of life" (John 6:68). The disciples could find no alternative to the life they had found in Jesus. The author of Hebrews also suggests that, while one may be carried away by new teachings, only Jesus Christ offers an "unshakable kingdom." There was, in fact, no alternative to Jesus Christ.

An amazing number of religions offer excitement, peace of mind, and a sense of adventure. At times, Christianity seems dull by comparison. But Hebrews reminds us that only Jesus Christ provides the security and permanence that we need.

We have also noticed that unique features of this book include arguments about the nature of Jesus Christ. We could dismiss these arguments as unimportant in an exhortation to a tired church. But the author of Hebrews insists that a church can survive only if its members "go on to maturity" (6:1) and receive "solid food" (5:14). This solid food includes an understanding of the words which the church confesses in corporate worship. It includes time devoted to examination and reflection on the meaning of the Bible. There is a place for explaining and exploring the meaning of the affirmations in the Bible. When we omit this maturing process, we are open to influences that cause us to drift away.

The "solid food" of Hebrews explains the identity of Jesus Christ. No book in the New Testament emphasizes both the humanity and exaltation of Jesus as much as Hebrews. The author describes Jesus as the "sympathetic high priest" (4:15), as the one who "learned obedience through suffering" (5:7-8), and as "our brother" (2:12-13). He also declares that Jesus is at God's right hand (1:3, 13; 8:1; 10:12) in heaven itself.

What place do such teachings have in a sermon on church renewal? Why did the author take time for such statements while trying to encourage his weary church. The reason for this insistence on showing both sides of Jesus' nature can be seen in a concept used more than once in Hebrews. According to 2:10 and 12:2, Jesus is our pioneer (*archēgos*). He has stood where we stand. He has made the journey already, and He has opened the way to God (10:19-23). This insistence on Jesus' humanity and divinity was not abstract speculation, but encouragement. It was the author's way of saying, "You do not need to drop out because you have a leader who knew all of your frustration, your weariness, and temptations. Now he has demonstrated that something lies ahead that makes your endurance worthwhile."

We also want to know if the struggle is worthwhile. When we think of Jesus as our pioneer, we know that He has shared our temptation to give up the struggle.

The author also insists that Jesus Christ is God's final word. According to the opening lines of the book, God has finally spoken completely through his Son. In other parts of the book, the author refers to this revelation in Jesus Christ as "once-for-all" (7:27, 9:28). Thus, whether Jesus is described as Son or high priest, we cannot mistake the message of Hebrews that there is no other way to salvation.

This claim has important implications for the survival of the church. If allegiance to Jesus Christ is only one option among many, there is no reason to pay the price of commitment. But if the direction of the cross is God's final expression of Himself, we have reason to continue. Hebrews 13 reminds us that Christian commitment may involve a lonely existence and the acceptance of values that are unpopular in our culture. Christ's death "outside the camp" reminds us that the Christian faith began with his enduring the agony and the shame of a death outside hallowed grounds. His endurance involved his acceptance of the unpopular way. So if Jesus Christ is God's final and unique revelation, we dare not try to revive the church by accommodating it to popular tastes. The church survives only by reaffirming its unique identity, its confession of faith, and its memory that the whole story began with the one who dared go "outside the camp."

"Hebrews reminds us that in Christ we have something too good to throw away.

We have observed also what is involved in giving up the faith. The author of Hebrews is so intent on reclaiming tired Christians that he reminds them that apostasy involves "recrucifying the Son of God" (6:6) and treating his sacrifice with contempt. It involves spurning the Son of God (10:26), profaning his blood, and outraging the Spirit of grace (10:26). We often take it as a casual matter when we consider whether to give up the faith or to remain Christian. Hebrews reminds us that in Christ we have something too good to throw away.

139

Our Response To God

When we look back over the history of the church, we can point to many factors that have probably allowed the church to survive adversity. The most important factor, of course, is the activity of God. God says in Isaiah 55:11,

So shall my word be that goes forth from my mouth;
it shall not return to me empty,
but it shall accomplish that which I purpose
and prosper in the thing for which I sent it.

However, there is another side of the story. The survival of the church also depends on people. In Ezekiel's vision of the dry bones (Ezek. 37), the breath of God brought life back to the people. But the labor of Ezekiel and the perseverance of others also led to the survival of the people of God. Survival depends, in large part, on the ability of the people of God to endure frustrations and doubts.

The message of Hebrews consists mainly of a reminder of the gifts that God granted us, but it does not stop here. The readers lived through the plundering of their property, and the imprisonment of many of their Christian friends (10:32-33), and the decline in church attendance (10:25). But they experienced a frustration they had not expected. In this situation there is no easy answer to a tired church. The author offers no magic solution to help the church survive in bad times. Instead, the author's advice consists in the simple call for his readers to "hold fast" and "persevere."

The author of Hebrews frequently offers this kind of advice. He assumes that Christian communities will experience discouragement. "We desire each one of you to show the same earnestness in realizing the full assurance of hope until the end" (6:11). "Let us hold fast the confession of hope without wavering" (10:23). The author tells his readers, "You have need of endurance" (10:36). "Let us run the race with perseverance," he says in a later passage (12:1).

In chapter 11 he recalls men and women who endured in bad times. He recalls that Jesus, our pioneer, "endured the cross" (12:2) before He was enthroned at God's right hand.

This advice to "persevere" or "hold fast" is not likely to be welcome for many of us. We like easy answers and quick solutions to our problems. We do not like to think that Christianity involves the difficulty of holding on in discouraging times. But Hebrews is a realistic book. The author surveys the history of God's people in chapters 3, 4, and 11, and recognizes that the heritage of faith has survived until his day because the heroes of the past endured in the struggle to believe. Now he knows that the future of faith depends on the ability of his people to endure.

The author's advice for his readers to "hold fast" is like the words of Old Testament prophets. They too knew the frustration of believing when they could see no signs of God's presence. In this situation, a characteristic word of the psalms and prophets is the simple advice to wait. "For thee I wait all the day long," the psalmist said (Psalms 25:5). In another passage, the psalmist says,

> Be still before the Lord, and wait patiently for him;
>   fret not yourself over him who prospers in his way,
>   over the man who carries out evil devices!
>   Psalms 37:7

The prophets frequently spoke to the discouraged people of God. Their call was an encouragement to wait.

> But they who wait for the Lord shall renew their strength,
>> they shall mount up with wings like eagles,
> they shall run and not be weary,
>> they shall walk and not faint.
>
> Isaiah 40:31

In our own times there have been occasions when commitment to the church was popular. We have seen times of dramatic growth and times of decline. It is easy to maintain commitment in times of rapid church growth because there is the encouragement of being associated with a popular cause. But Christian commitment is more difficult when the church has lost its popularity. The church today is deeply indebted to those who persevered in past generations when the cause appeared to be lost. We also owe much today to those people like Elijah who went on with the business of faith when it looked as if the numbers had dwindled to nothing. Future generations will also be indebted to those who held on in times of discouragement. Therefore, the survival of the church depends not only on God. It depends also on those people who go on providing encouragement to others, teaching classes, and helping with the various ministries of the church. Without those who commit themselves to such responsibilities, there would be no renewal.

Responsible For Each Other

It is not easy to "hold fast" in a culture which accepts ideals different from our own, as we observed in chapter 12. Hebrews contains a strong emphasis on the community of believers as a resource for revitalizing the church. A Christian may experience the loneliness of holding to truths which others find unacceptable, but the Christian is also supported by a whole community of believers who live "outside the camp." The community goes on this pilgrimage together.

We recognize this emphasis on the whole community when the author says, "Take care, brethren, lest there be in any of you an evil, unbelieving heart, leading you to fall away from the living God. But exhort one another every day, . . . that none of you may be hardened by the deceitfulness of sin" (3:12-13). The work of caring for the community is not reserved for a few leaders. The whole church is addressed here. Also, there is an emphasis on words like "any" and "none." The church is on a pilgrimage together. As it proceeds, it is careful that no one drops out along the way. It is a community of people who encourage one another each day.

"The pilgrim people of God are responsible for each other."

This emphasis on encouragement is the important issue later in the book when the author exhorts his community about attendance at worship. Christians "encourage one another" (10:25) during group worship.

Hebrews 12:12-17 emphasizes the responsibility of Christians for each other. It is not enough for Christians to maintain their commitment. But the author reminds Christians of their responsibility for others. They are to make "straight paths" along the way so that no one is injured. They are to see to it that "no one" fails to attain the grace of God or, like Esau, gets caught up in false values. The pilgrim people of God are responsible for each other.

The church today struggles with the same problem that confronted the people of God in the Old Testament and the church in its second generation. Others before us have asked, "Will the Son of Man find faith on the earth?" We have found one way of answering this problem from our study of Hebrews. The book points us to the greatness of God's final revelation in his Son. It reminds us that we have received in Jesus Christ a gift that is too precious to throw away. And it reminds us that the answer to the question also depends on our willingness to follow our pioneer who "endured the cross."